Air Heroes of World War II

Robert Jackson

Air Heroes of
World War II

Sixteen Stories of Heroism in the Air

ST. MARTINS PRESS   NEW YORK

Library of Congress Cataloging in Publication Data

Jackson, Robert, 1941–
    Air heroes of World War II.

    1. World War, 1939–1945—Aerial operations.
2. World War, 1939–1945—Biography. I. Title.
D785.J318   940.54'4'0922   [B]   77–18382
ISBN 0–312–01516–x

Contents

Introduction

THE STORY OF THE SECOND WORLD WAR IS THE
story of ordinary people performing extraordinary feats,
often with great courage.

Nowhere was this more true than in the air, where
technical troubles and the weather caused as many problems as the enemy.

This book tells of courage in the air, from a valiant
low-level attack by RAF bombers on the German fleet on
the second day of the war to a suicidal, lone dive against
a Japanese destroyer by a navy pilot when the war was
almost over.

The stories in between show courage in all its mani-
festations. The Russian pilot who crawled through the
snow for nineteen days with no feet; the men who risked
their lives night after night in flimsy aircraft to land
agents in occupied Europe; the film star who saved an
American bomber squadron from destruction; the German pilot who ordered ss officers from his aircraft at
gunpoint in order to save wounded soldiers; French
bomber crews who had the agonizing task of bombing
their own capital city – all these and other true tales tell
of men who became heroes in their own way, in the sky
between 1939 and 1945.

Illustrations

FIRST
STRIKE

When World War II broke out, the RAF lost no time in getting to grips with the enemy. On the second day of the war, Blenheims of RAF Bomber Command set out on a gallant daylight mission against one of the most heavily defended targets in Germany.

THE LONE BRISTOL BLENHEIM RECONNAISSANCE aircraft dropped down through the clouds that sheltered the German naval base at Wilhelmshaven. The pilot opened the throttles and the aircraft skimmed over the Schillig Roads, its cameras whirring. Ten minutes later it was roaring over the Elbe Estuary. His job well done, the pilot climbed back into the shelter of the clouds.

Not a shot had been fired. It was the morning of 4 September 1939, and Britain had been at war with Germany for less than twenty-four hours.

At noon the Blenheim landed at Wyton, in Huntingdonshire, and the exposed films were hurriedly developed. The RAF intelligence officers who examined the still wet plates could hardly believe their eyes. In the Schillig Roads lay a huge battleship, surrounded by an armada of light cruisers and destroyers. It was the *Admiral Scheer*. That wasn't all: riding at anchor on the Elbe were the battle-cruisers *Scharnhorst* and *Gneisenau*.

It was too good a target to miss. Here was a golden chance for RAF Bomber Command to strike a crippling blow at the German battle fleet on the second day of the war.

At Wattisham, in Suffolk, sweating ground crews worked flat out to load the Blenheim bombers of Nos 107 and 110 Squadrons with armour-piercing bombs. They had just finished the job when somebody decided that the attack would have to be made at low level to escape the worst of the fire from the warships' heavy anti-aircraft guns, and armour-piercing bombs were no use unless they were dropped from a fairly high altitude. So the cursing crews had to start all over again and replace the armour-piercing bombs with ordinary 500-pounders, fitted with eleven-second fuses. It was the fifth time the bomb-loads had been changed in twenty-four hours.

At last everything was ready. Only the very best would do for this job, and ten crews were carefully selected – five from 107 Squadron and five from 110.

It was just on four o'clock when, one by one, the Blenheims roared down Wattisham's runway and lifted into the air. Led by Flight Lieutenant Ken Doran, they sped over the coast and set course eastward, flying in two tight formations of five.

At about the same time, a further flight of five Blenheims was taking off from Wyton, and an hour later twelve Hampdens – six from 49 Squadron and six from 83 – left Scampton in Lincolnshire. None of these aircraft was destined to find the target. After cruising around for hours on end, hopelessly lost in thick cloud and fog, they were forced to return to their bases.

As the ten Blenheims from Wattisham droned on, Doran noticed that the cloud base was getting steadily lower. The sky was heavily overcast, and a strong norwester blew the rainclouds over the North Sea in towards the German coast.

Soon, the Blenheims were flying in a narrow 300-foot gap between the cloud base and the heaving grey sea. Sometimes they came as low as fifty feet. The clouds formed a solid wall right up to 20,000 feet. It was a nerve-racking business, flying over the sea at this height. A false move would be fatal. Hitting the water at 200 mph would be about as soft as flying into a brick wall. But it was their only chance of finding the target.

Doran peered ahead into the murk, running over the attack plan in his mind. At the briefing they had been told that the German pocket battleships were armed with only two types of anti-aircraft weapons: heavy guns and machine-guns. The idea was to go in low where the heavy guns could not be brought to bear on them. They were to spread out and attack from three directions, to confuse the gunners. The bombs were supposed to lodge in the ship's superstructure, where they would go off after a delay of eleven seconds. This meant that the pilots who made their bomb-runs after the leader would have to go in with split-second timing, otherwise there was a very real danger that they would be blown sky-high by the explosions of the bombs dropped by the preceding aircraft.

One other thing: if they were unable to attack the warships, they were to bomb the ammunition depot at Marienhof as a secondary target. Under no circumstances were they to endanger civilian lives by bombing the dockyard. The orders were quite definite about that.

Doran glanced at his watch. In ten seconds it would be time to turn. He hoped to God that his navigation had been good. There were no landmarks in this featureless vista of sea and cloud.

The formation altered course towards the south-east, heading for the north coast of Germany. Rain streamed down the bombers' windscreens in rivulets. Once a couple of trawlers flashed beneath their wings and were immediately swallowed up in the fog behind them.

Suddenly there was land. An island slid by to starboard, and ahead was a coastline broken by a wide bay. Doran had to look twice before he realized that it was the Jade estuary. They were exactly on target.

The Blenheims roared on, heading straight for Wilhelmshaven. Amazingly, the weather began to clear a little. The rain stopped and the cloud base lifted perceptibly higher, to about 500 feet.

Dead ahead, a long dark shape rose out of the water. It was the *Admiral Scheer*.

Doran flicked the r/t switch. No point in keeping radio silence now.

'Numbers four and five, break! attack, attack!'

Led by Doran, the first three Blenheims roared flat out towards the battleship. The other two aircraft broke to left and right and shot up into the clouds.

On board the *Scheer* everything was normal. The sailors were going about their routine duties. From his lofty platform high up in front of the foremast, the flak control officer stared out across the grey water at the misty outlines of the neighbouring destroyers.

A sudden shout over the intercom jerked him into action.

'Number Four anti-aircraft position here, sir. Three aircraft bearing one-nine-o.'

The officer raised his binoculars and scanned the sky astern of the ship. Three black dots were racing along just below the clouds, getting bigger every second. Twin engines, single fins. They looked like Junkers 88s. The officer swore. How often had those Luftwaffe idiots to be warned not to fly over the Fleet? One day, someone with an itchy trigger-finger was going to give them a hot reception.

A yell from one of the lookouts shattered his thoughts.

'Sir – those aren't ours! They're Blenheims!' The Tommies are here.'

The strident blare of the klaxon resounded through the ship as the leading Blenheim bored in, thrumming steadily on above the waves. Hunched in the cockpit, Doran grimly held his course as the great battle-wagon loomed up in front of him. He could see what looked like a line of washing strung across the after-deck. There was a hazy impression of white upturned faces. Some of the sailors waved. Then they saw the red, white and blue roundels stamped on the Blenheim's wings and scattered in all directions.

'Bombs away!'

Doran hauled back the stick as his navigator pressed the bomb-release. The grey superstructure shot past terrifyingly close beneath the aircraft. The two 500-pounders dropped away and curved down towards the *Scheer*. One burrowed its way into the superstructure, the other bounced off the armoured deck and fell into the sea.

Neither of them exploded.

The anti-aircraft gunners had woken up at last, and the *Scheer's* sombre hull twinkled with flashes as the ship's 20-millimetre twin-barrelled cannon – the cannon that German pocket battleships were not supposed to have – sent streams of glowing shells after the twisting aircraft. Doran raced for safety, so low that the slipstream from the engines fanned twin furrows on the surface of the water.

The second Blenheim came sliding in, the pilot threading his way through a wall of dirty black shell-bursts. One of his bombs raised a thunderous fountain of water near the *Scheer's* side; the other, like Doran's, never exploded.

The dull sky was suddenly filled with brilliant light as the ships let fly with everything they had. Multi-coloured tracers arced up into the clouds from the barrels of more than a hundred guns. Heavy batteries on the shore opened up with a vicious thud.

Halfway through his run-in, the pilot of the third Blenheim suddenly pulled up into the clouds. He was obeying his instructions: he knew that he could not bomb within the eleven-second time limit.

A blazing ball tumbled out of the clouds and smacked into the sea near Mellum Island. It was one of the diversionary Blenheims, caught in the meshes of the flak.

There was a momentary respite. The echoes died away and a haze of smoke drifted slowly over the water.

Then a fresh alarm, as the five aircraft of 107 Squadron came roaring in from the north-west. They ran smack into the combined fire of every gun in and around the anchorage. The leading Blenheim, caught in a murderous cross-fire from at least thirty 20-millimetres, simply disappeared. One moment it was there, the next it had vanished. Blazing fragments fell hissing into the sea from a spreading cloud of oily smoke. The second, streaming flame from both engines, crashed on the deck of the cruiser *Emden,* killing the first German sailors of the war. The third, dragging a long banner of grey smoke, climbed almost vertically towards the clouds, stalled and crashed near the shore. The fourth, bracketed by a cluster of heavy shells, cartwheeled over the water and subsided in a tangled heap of wreckage. The fifth somehow got through the barrage unscathed, dropped its bombs in a beautiful straddle across the *Scheer,* and vanished in the overcast. Again, the bomb that hit the battleship failed to explode.

As the surviving Blenheims droned away into the distance, a heavy silence fell over the bay. A cloud of smoke hung over the *Emden,* where a river of fuel from the crashed Blenheim's tanks still burned.

Altogether, three bombs had hit the *Scheer.* Every one had been a dud. The attack had failed because of useless bombs: old bombs, stored too long in poor conditions. The price of failure had been five aircraft and fifteen men.

Doran's part in the attack brought him the award of the Distinguished Flying Cross, the first to be won in World War II. He and his crews had struck the first blow against the enemy, but they had learned a bitter lesson.

It was going to be a long, hard struggle. Courage alone was not going to see it through.

BATTLE IN
THE WINTER

Among all the stories of heroism in the years from 1939 to 1945, none stands more highly than the struggle of tiny Finland against Russia. This is the story of a Finnish fighter pilot during the Winter War, a man who, day after day, hurled himself into battle against incredible odds.

LIKE A SWARM OF HORNETS, THE NINE AIRCRAFT crawled across the blue backdrop of the sky, the light reflected from the snow glittering palely on their bellies. They were Dutch-built Fokker D.21 fighters, and on the brown camouflage of their wings and fuselages they bore the markings of the Finnish Air Force – a blue swastika within a white circle.

From the cockpit of the third machine in the second flight, Lieutenant Jorma Sarvanto scanned the snow-covered landscape below. It was a scene of great beauty, but Sarvanto's face was tense and grim. For this was 19 December 1939, and for nineteen days Finland had been at war with Russia. For nineteen days, the tiny Finnish Army had fought bitterly and heroically in the heart of the lovely forests, and, incredibly, had managed to bring the red floodtide to a standstill.

Ahead of them now, as they approached the front line near Summa, the pilots of the 24th Squadron could see war's ugly signpost staining the sky: smoke, drifting from burning farms. The virgin snow began to be pock-marked with dirty craters. Greasy tufts of yellow smoke from the Russian anti-aircraft batteries drifted past, well below the Finnish formation.

Suddenly, there was a flicker of movement against the snow. Half a dozen pilots saw it at once, and identified it:

an old Russian Polikarpov R-5 biplane, no doubt employed as an artillery spotter. A section of four Fokkers
peeled off and hurtled down on the unsuspecting enemy.
A brief flurry of machine-gun fire, and the R-5's flaming
wreckage was scattered over the snow. The Fokkers
climbed up to rejoin the others and resumed their patrol.

The minutes ticked by. Not a sign of a Russian aircraft.
Fuel was getting dangerously low. Reluctantly, the pilots
turned and set course for their base at Kakisalmi.

Suddenly a warning shout crackled over the R/T:
'Enemy bombers above, to the left!' There they were,
nine Tupolev SB-2 twin-engined bombers, the sun glinting on their wings as they came into view above a bank
of cloud which had blown up out of the west.

Sarvanto slammed his throttle wide open and climbed
to meet the enemy. Stick hard over, a kick on the rudder-
bar and he was swinging in behind the Russian formation
as it slid past him. A SB-2 drifted into his sights and he
fired, seeing his bullets flash and sparkle on the enemy's
dark green wings. Tracer lanced past the Fokker's cockpit
and Sarvanto hauled back the stick frantically, the little
fighter bounding skywards as though on elastic. Sweating,
he stall-turned and dived vertically on the bomber which
had fired at him. For a split second the SB-2 seemed to
hang motionless, spreadeagled in his sights. A quick burst,
and then he was hurtling past, terrifyingly close. A glance
to the rear: the bomber was nosing earthwards, blazing
furiously.

The SB-2s crammed on power and turned towards the
front line. One of them, trailing a thin stream of smoke
from his starboard engine, began to lag behind the rest.
Sarvanto closed in and fired at point-blank range, killing
the rear-gunner. The pilot jettisoned his bomb load and
twisted away from the Fokker's bullets. Grimly, Sarvanto
clung to his tail and fired again. The SB-2 skidded and

lost height. Desperately, the pilot levelled out and tried to ditch his aircraft on Lake Vuoksa. At the last moment, the SB-2's wingtip ploughed into the ice and the bomber cartwheeled in a cloud of fragments.

Sarvanto had no time to congratulate himself. With his fuel almost gone, he just managed to reach an emergency landing strip, where toiling airmen refuelled his Fokker for the flight back to Kakisalmi.

On Christmas Eve the squadron moved to Vuoksenlaakso, near the spot where Sarvanto had destroyed his second victim a few days before. Christmas morning dawned red and bitterly cold, with a cutting north wind whispering in the pine trees round the frozen lake which the squadron used as its base. Snow drifted down as the mechanics swarmed round the Fokkers, while the duty pilots sat huddled round the stove in the crew-tent, drinking scalding coffee. From time to time, the muted rumble of heavy guns reached them.

The sky grew steadily lighter. A sudden yell from outside startled the pilots into action: vapour trails had been sighted, apparently heading for Vuoksenlaakso. Coffee forgotten, they dashed for their aircraft, cursing as the full impact of the icy air hit them. A Mercury engine started up with a crackling roar, followed by another and another. Sarvanto slammed shut the cockpit canopy and pushed the throttle open. The Fokker tore across the makeshift airfield in a cloud of snow just as the first bombs erupted on the shore.

Sarvanto climbed hell for leather and looked round: the original enemy had vanished. He circled, scanning the horizon, the whole of Karelia spread out beneath his wings. As luck would have it, his engine began to misfire badly just as six SB-2s slid into view beneath him, over Nuijamaa Lake. Sarvanto juggled with the throttle and decided to attack, half-rolling and diving on the enemy.

They jettisoned their bombs haphazardly and fled. Sarvanto turned for home, his engine spluttering and the cockpit rapidly filling with smoke. Later, the squadron mechanics found that the intense cold had cracked a piston.

By the New Year, the 24th Squadron's score had risen to 100 Russian aircraft destroyed. On 3 January the Squadron was ordered to move west to Utti, on the Russian bombers' main route to targets in central Finland.

On 6 January, Sarvanto was flying a lone patrol over the devastated town of Mikkeli when he spotted a formation of seven Ilyushin DB-3 bombers. He climbed at full throttle and attacked out of the sun, closing in rapidly on the rearmost flight of three enemy bombers. A gentle pressure on the rudder bar brought him in line with the bomber on the extreme left of the formation, and he fought to hold the Fokker steady as she hit the Russians' slipstream. The enemy gunners had spotted him at last, and smoky trails zipped past his cockpit. Bullets tore through the wings of the fighter, but Sarvanto held on and closed the range to fifty yards.

A long, hammering burst from the Fokker's guns and suddenly the Russian's starboard wing became a mass of flame. The DB-3 slewed out of formation and spun down towards the white snowscape in a mushroom of smoke. Sarvanto shifted his attention to the next DB-3 in line, watching his bullets chew up the Russian's starboard engine cowling. A bright flicker, and then a river of flame shot back from the engine. The bomber followed its companion in a last plunge earthwards.

Frantically, Sarvanto flung his fighter away from the deadly cone of fire which threatened to ensnare him. As he did so, the pale blue belly of a DB-3 filled his sights for a fraction of a second. It was enough. A quick jab on the gun-button and his bullets stitched a jagged seam up the bomber's fuselage. The DB-3 faltered, a wing dropped and it fell, turning over and over.

Three down! Sarvanto drew off a little and calmly selected his next victim. He closed in again and fired, and a fourth DB-3 went into a spin, its rudder shot away. A few seconds later it was joined by a fifth, the crew dead in the bullet-shattered cockpit.

The sixth bomber banked into the sun in a desperate effort to escape. Sarvanto noticed the manoeuvre and turned to intercept. The pilot of this DB-3 was no novice: he tried every trick in the book to get away from the fighter worrying at his tail. It was no use. Controls shot away, the bomber went into a tight spiral and crashed in a fountain of snow and earth.

Sarvanto chased the seventh Russian, who was diving hard towards the Russian lines. He crept within range and pressed the button: nothing happened. He was out of ammunition. Swearing, he reluctantly turned away and set course for Utti, practically out of fuel, his fighter riddled like a colander. He glanced at his watch: the fight had lasted a bare five minutes.

A short while later, as Sarvanto was recounting the details of his fight to a crowd of jubilant mechanics, two more Fokkers slid to a standstill on the frozen lake. The grinning pilots – Lieutenant Sovelius and Sergeant Ikonen – hoisted themselves from the cockpits and joined the small crowd. It turned out that they had seen the whole fight, but had been too far away to get there in time. However, that seventh Russian had not been so lucky after all. They had caught him as he was crossing the lines and shot him to pieces.

January wore on. Day after day, in bitter cold, the Finnish pilots took off from their frozen lakes in worn-out aircraft and flung themselves tirelessly on the Russian formations. At the beginning of February, Jorma Sarvanto was promoted to command a flight of the 24th Squadron.

On 15th February, the squadron was over the Russian lines when suddenly it was 'bounced' by an avalanche of enemy fighters. The sky quickly became a whirling confusion of white-painted I-153s and dark green I-16s. Sarvanto found himself isolated in the middle of a melee of Russians, but managed to get away in a steep climb. Below him, the twisting aircraft looked like flies against the snowy background.

A red-nosed I-16 sped past, a couple of hundred feet below. Sarvanto went after him in a shallow dive. Just before he fired, Sarvanto glanced rearwards as a matter of habit. It was just as well he did: two I-153s were sitting on his tail, about to finish him off. He pulled back the stick and shot skywards, losing both his pursuers and his erstwhile target.

Far below, a Fokker was diving towards Lake Saimaa, trailing a thin streamer of smoke, an I-153 hot on its tail. Sarvanto dived to help, but his Fokker suddenly shuddered as bullets ripped into its starboard wing. An I-153 was close behind him, blazing away. The Fokker dropped into a spin and Sarvanto worked the controls to bring her out as the earth gyrated around him. It was no use; the Fokker continued to tumble out of the sky like a falling leaf. He had to get out, quickly. He reached for the hood release handle, and at that precise moment the Fokker came out of the spin by itself. Sarvanto had had enough; there was no telling what damage the Russian's bullets had done. He raced for home flat out, a few hundred feet above the snow.

Four days later, on the nineteenth, Sarvanto was leading his Flight on a patrol near Lapeenranta when he spotted a cluster of black dots away to the east. The dots grew rapidly bigger until they resolved themselves into the shapes of twenty-seven DB-3s and an escort of ten I-16 fighters. As Sarvanto was making up his mind whether to attack or not, more friendly fighters arrived on the scene and hurled themselves on the I-16s.

Under cover of the diversion, Sarvanto's four aircraft climbed to intercept the bombers. The enemy formation saw them coming and pulled up into a layer of cloud a few thousand feet above. Ice began to form on the Fokkers' wings as the pilots plunged into the cloud after them. Suddenly, a huge, ghostly shape loomed up in front of Sarvanto. He had flown smack into the middle of the Russian formation. His tracers lit up the murk as he fired. Lurid sparks bounced from the DB-3's wings and it turned slowly over on its back and dropped out of sight. At the same moment a Fokker plunged past, minus a wing and blazing furiously.

Sarvanto could not see a thing. He was bound to collide with something at any second. He dived free of the cloud and turned south, spotting a formation of eight DBs slipping away towards the Gulf of Finland as he did so. He could have caught up with them easily, but as he was low in fuel and ammunition he let them go.

Russian fighters roamed the sky of Finland freely now, outnumbering the defenders by ten to one. A number of Finnish pilots were shot down while landing or taking off by hit-and-run enemy fighters. The Russians, having suffered crippling losses at the hands of their much smaller opponent, were now hitting the Finnish airfields with everything they had.

On 26 February, the 24th Squadron was ordered back to its original base at Kakisalmi. The end was not far away now. The army was still holding on valiantly against overwhelming enemy forces, but the position was worsening every day. Then came an opportunity the Finnish pilots had been waiting for. The Russians were attempting to land a large force from the ice near Virolahti, and were being routed by artillery fire. The 24th Squadron was ordered into action against the disorganized enemy.

Roaring low across the coast under a blanket of cloud, the pilots dived on the tangled columns of men and horses, guns hammering. The slaughter was frightful. Streams of bullets ricocheted across the ice, mowing down the enemy in great swathes. The Russians broke and fled, trampling their wounded comrades into the bloodstained snow.

The Russians tried again, this time on the northern shore of Viipuri Bay. Soon the ice was littered with corpses, strewn among the carcasses of burnt-out tanks. Twenty Fokkers dived on the survivors, lighting up the mist with the glare of darting tracers. It was getting difficult to see; dusk was falling, pierced by the glow from burning Russian transports. Suddenly a squadron of I-153s tumbled out of the gloom and the Fokkers, out of ammunition, fled for home.

For days the massacre went on. For days the Russians stubbornly tried to smash through the Finnish defences and were slaughtered in their thousands. They lay in heaps on the ice, their blood freezing in the cold. Above the carnage the fighters roared endlessly, diving and strafing. The world held its breath as tiny Finland smashed the mighty Russian Bear to its knees again and again.

But it was the last act of the drama. On 12 March the armistice was signed and the Winter War came to an end.

Frustrated by the Armistice, the Finnish airmen looked to the east and longed for revenge. They had fought the Russians, and they had smashed them. In the beginning they had been promised help by several nations, but only a trickle of new equipment had begun to arrive a week or two before the end, when it was too late.

In every Finnish airman's heart was a bitter feeling of betrayal. Yet who could he blame? He knew only that he had done his best, and more than his best. For his comrades who had given all there was to give, what better tribute than the words of people who stopped him in the street and said: 'We saw the part you played. You fought like men!'

BATTLE OVER NORWAY

In April 1940, the German invasion of Norway brought the 'Phoney War' period to an abrupt end. The Stukas and Heinkels were everywhere, relentlessly bombing the Allies as they fought desperately among the mountains. To oppose them, the RAF could spare only one squadron – equipped with outdated Gloster Gladiator biplane fighters. Nevertheless, their pilots were to write one of the most gallant chapters in the annals of air fighting.

AT SIX O'CLOCK IN THE EVENING OF 24 APRIL, eighteen Gloster Gladiators of No. 263 Squadron, RAF, landed on the frozen surface of Lake Lesjaskog, about forty miles from Aandalsnes, in Norway. Two days previously, on the twenty-second, 263's pilots had flown their aircraft aboard the aircraft carrier HMS *Glorious*, at Scapa Flow. Only then had they been told their destination.

On 9 April 1940, eight months after the end of the Polish Campaign, the Germans had suddenly attacked on a second front – not in France, as the Allies had expected, but in Norway.

For two weeks, the tiny Norwegian Army, aided by an expeditionary force of British, French and Polish troops, had been battling desperately against overwhelming odds. The Norwegian Air Arm had been quickly destroyed, leaving the Allied ground forces without air cover until the arrival of No. 263's Gladiators.

Conditions at Lesjaskog were frightful. A handful of airmen strove all night to refuel and arm the Gladiators, working in sub-zero temperatures. When dawn broke, they found that the carburettors and control surfaces were frozen solid. Nevertheless, they managed to get two Gladiators airworthy, and these two took off just before five in the morning to patrol over the lake.

Trouble was not long in coming, in the shape of a Heinkel 115 seaplane. The Gladiators attacked it and shot it down. Under cover of the diversion, a Heinkel 111 slipped across the lake and unloaded a stick of bombs, but without doing any damage.

All that morning, the Gladiators maintained constant patrols, in support of the Army, often taking off from the lake between bomb-bursts and streams of machine-gun fire. No. 263 suffered its first loss at eleven when a Gladiator was destroyed on the ground by a low-flying Heinkel. The pilot, Sergeant Forrest, had just got clear of the aircraft. In the space of an hour, nine more Gladiators had been destroyed, all on the ground, in exchange for one He.111 shot down by Flight Lieutenant Mills. At noon, an intruding He.111 was attacked by a section of Gladiators led by Pilot Officer McNamara. The Heinkel went into a spin and crashed on the edge of the lake. A column of black smoke, tinged with balls of flame, marked its grave.

Early that afternoon, the surviving Gladiators shot down another Heinkel and badly hit its companion, which limped away streaming smoke. Not long afterwards, Squadron Leader J. W. Donaldson and Flight Lieutenant Mills caught a Heinkel near Aandalsnes and shot it down into a ravine. That evening, Mills got mixed up in a running fight with half a dozen Junkers 88s. Out of fuel and ammunition, he had to make a forced landing, and he had just finished surveying the bullet holes in his battle-worn Gladiator's wings and fuselage when two He.111s roared across and blasted it to shreds.

When darkness fell, the surface of Lake Lesjaskog was pitted and torn by countless bomb-craters. Only four Gladiators were left now, and these were evacuated to Aandalsnes.

The following morning, Pilot Officer Craig-Adams took

off on a reconnaissance sortie. He had been flying for about ten minutes when the Gladiator's worn-out Mercury engine seized up with a clatter. Craig-Adams bailed out and made his way safely back to Aandalsnes.

It was the end. On 27 April the last fuel supplies ran out. The next day, the pilots received the order to destroy their remaining aircraft. Bitterly, they watched the last three faithful Gladiators go up in flames. That evening they embarked on the cargo vessel *Delius*, and, after running the gauntlet through several dive-bombing attacks off the Norwegian coast, they reached Scapa Flow on 1 May without further incident.

On 14 May No. 263 – now re-equipped with eighteen Gladiator IIs – sailed into action once more aboard HMS *Glorious*. This time the destination was Bardufoss, near Narvik, and the Squadron's task was to support the Allied Forces' Second Norwegian Expedition.

Misfortune struck the Squadron before it even reached Norway. On 21 May, two sections of Gladiators – each section led by a Fleet Air Arm Swordfish – took off from the flight deck of *Glorious* in a blinding, gale-driven storm of sleet. The pilots soon realized that they did not have a hope of reaching Bardufoss in weather like this, and turned back. One section found the carrier again, and, in spite of almost zero visibility, miraculously managed to land safely on the heaving deck. The other section was not so lucky. The leading Swordfish, hopelessly lost, flew straight into the side of a fog-shrouded mountain at Soreisa. A split second later, it was followed by two Gladiators. Pilot Officer Richards was killed instantly and Flight Lieutenant Mills was badly injured in the crash. The wreckage of the three aircraft blazed on the barren mountainside, three forlorn beacons glowing redly through the murk.

An advance force of eight Gladiators finally reached

Bardufoss on 22 May, and was immediately flung into action.

Pilot Officer Craig-Adams was the first to die in air combat. What happened is not clear: it appears that, having run out of ammunition, he deliberately rammed a Heinkel 111. The wreckage of the two aircraft was found side by side, with the body of Craig-Adams still strapped in the cockpit of his Gladiator.

The remaining Gladiators flew in the next day, making a total of fourteen airworthy fighters. The same day, Sergeant Whall shot down a Dornier 17 after a scrap lasting twenty-five minutes: a few moments later he ran out of fuel himself and had to bail out.

On the morning of the twenty-fourth, four Messerschmitt 110s strafed the airfield. They were met with highly accurate anti-aircraft fire, and, after a couple of passes, drew off to a safe distance and circled watchfully. Flying Officer Grant Ede took off and attacked the enemy formation single-handed, and after a brisk exchange of fire, the Messerschmitts dived away and disappeared.

Ede was airborne again that afternoon. With Flying Officer Riley, he caught a lone Heinkel 111 flying at 500 feet over Bardufoss. He slammed home a burst, killing the enemy rear gunner, then half-rolled away. Riley attacked in turn, putting the Heinkel's starboard engine out of action. A third Gladiator, flown by Flight Lieutenant C. B. Hull, dropped into the fight and riddled the bomber's port motor. The Heinkel slewed round in a diving turn and crash-landed near Salanger. The crew were taken prisoner.

Success came Ede's way again early the following morning. Returning from a patrol, he spotted a big four-engined Junkers 90 transport cruising along at 15,000 feet north of Harstadt. He closed in and fired two bursts at long range. It was a lucky shot: the Junkers 90 went into a shallow dive and crash-landed in the sea off Dyroy Island. Ede caught a second Junkers 90 on another sortie later that day. His first burst killed the rear gunner, and he systematically shot each of the transport's four engines out of action. The Junkers burst into flames and it crashed on Finnoen Island, south of Narvik. A third Junkers 90 was shot down that evening near Harstadt by Pilot Officer Purdy and Sergeant Kitchener.

The next day, the twenty-sixth, saw 263 Squadron engaged in some bitter air fighting. During one of the first sorties, Flight Lieutenant Williams and Sergeant Milligan pounced on a Junkers 88 over Skaanland and shot it to ribbons. Later, a section of three Gladiators, flown by Flight Lieutenant Hull, Lieutenant Lydekker (a Fleet Air Arm pilot) and Pilot Officer Falkson was detached to the airstrip at Bodo, close to the battle-line. Hull attacked a Heinkel 111 over Salte Fjord and the enemy bomber fled with one engine burning. Turning away from the chase, Hull spotted a Junkers 52/3m transport flying in formation with another Heinkel 111. The Heinkel turned tail and Hull shot down the Junkers in flames. Two more Heinkels appeared, but put down their noses and ran for it when Hull bored in to the attack. Swearing, Hull looked round. A short distance away, and slightly below, two Junkers 52s were slipping towards the shelter of a bank of cloud. Hull attacked, using up the last of the ammunition for his wing guns. One of the Junkers spun into the ground, blazing fiercely; the other reached the cloud and vanished.

Half the Luftwaffe was airborne today! Hull pushed the stick over, kicked the rudder-bar and dived on a Heinkel III which had suddenly come into view. Only one of Hull's nose Brownings was working, yet he sent the Heinkel packing with smoke trailing from one engine.

34

His fuel dangerously low, Hull flew back to Bodo, where he landed just before nightfall.

Meanwhile, back at Bardufoss, it had been a hectic day for the rest of 263 Squadron. Some vicious fighting had taken place over Harstadt when Pilot Officers Purdy and Bentley attacked six Dornier 17s and shot down one each, subsequently driving off the others. On a later patrol over Harstadt, Flying Officer Riley and Pilot Officer Parnall came upon a formation of Heinkel 111s, which they attacked. Two Heinkels went down in flames, but Riley was wounded in the neck and hands.

Early on the morning of the twenty-seventh, a mixed formation of fourteen Junkers 87 'Stukas' and Messerschmitt 110s swept over Bodo airstrip and began to bomb and strafe the town's small harbour. Hull and Lydekker ran for their aircraft, roared off and tore into the fray. Each shot down a Junkers 87; then a Messerschmitt 110 got on Hull's tail and pumped a burst of cannon-fire into the Gladiator. Splinters knifed into Hull's head and knee. Bleeding profusely and barely conscious, he turned away and made a forced landing in the hills. It was destined to be Hull's last fight in Norway: two days later, he was evacuated to England. He cursed his luck at the time. A couple of weeks later, he would have cause to bless it.

Lydekker was also wounded in the neck and shoulder, and broke off the action. With Messerschmitts swarming like hornets over Bodo, he limped the 100 miles north to Bardufoss, where he crash-landed. His Gladiator was a total wreck.

The Luftwaffe made few sorties into 263's sector during the next five days, and the exhausted pilots and ground crews were able to snatch a few hours' well-earned rest. The only successful combat took place on the twenty-eighth, when Flight Lieutenant Williams caught a Heinkel 111 attacking shipping in Ofot Fjord and drove it off with both engines pouring smoke. During this week of comparative respite, the Squadron flew about thirty sorties against ground targets, one of which was the German Army Headquarters at Hundalen.

On 2 June General Auchinleck, commanding the Allied Expeditionary Force, gave orders for evacuation. Immediately, the Luftwaffe flung its whole might against the harassed Allied troops. No. 263 Squadron – now assisted by No. 46 Squadron, flying Hurricanes from Skaanland – flew a total of fifty-five sorties that day against the massed enemy formations. By noon, the Squadron's score stood at four Heinkels and a Junkers 87.

At half-past two in the afternoon, Pilot Officers Jacobsen and Wilkie were patrolling the narrow corridor between Narvik and Sweden when they encountered a pair of Junkers 88s. Jacobsen dived on the enemy from the beam, guns hammering. Wilkie followed suit, attacking from astern, but the Ju.88's rear gunner was ready for him. Riddled with bullets, his Gladiator went into a spin and crashed. The Ju.88 fled into a bank of cloud over the Swedish border.

Jacobsen turned and pounced on the second Junkers, which went into a vertical dive and vanished in the low cloud. As he was only flying at 500 feet, and the terrain below was stiff with mountains, it was unlikely that he would have been able to pull out.

Jacobsen climbed at full throttle and looked around. Suddenly he ran smack into a mixed formation of Junkers and Heinkels. A Heinkel slid across his nose and he got in a good solid burst. The bomber stalled, flicked over on its wingtip and blew up on the ground near Bjornfjell.

A Junkers 88 and three Heinkels roared at him, head on, blazing away with their nose guns. Jacobsen pulled up sharply and ripped off a three-second burst into a

Heinkel. The bomber spiralled earthwards, apparently out of control.

The Gladiator shuddered as heavy-calibre machine-gun bullets smacked into it. Oil spurted over the windscreen. Through it, Jacobsen saw the shadowy outline of yet another Heinkel. He fired, using up the last of his ammunition. Greedy flames licked over the bomber's wings and it nosed over, trailing a banner of smoke.

Hotly pursued by the other enemy aircraft, Jacobsen fled for home. When he reached base, having shaken off his pursuers by some brilliant low flying, he was so tired he could hardly climb from the cockpit.

Later, Jacobsen was credited with three enemy aircraft destroyed. His score during that magnificent single-handed fight may probably, in actual fact, have been higher.

It was the final round. On 7 June the Norwegian Campaign drew to a close, and the Gladiators flew their last patrol, during which they shot down three more bombers. Then they set course out over the sea, heading for the *Glorious*. Together with the surviving Hurricanes of 46 Squadron, they all landed safely as dusk was falling. For the last time, the *Glorious* pointed her bow away from Norway, towards Scapa Flow.

On the afternoon of 8 June 1940, *Glorious* was caught in the open sea by the German battle-cruisers *Scharnhorst* and *Gneisenau*. In a running fight lasting less than two hours, the cruisers pumped salvo after salvo into the carrier. At last, tiredly, she turned over and slid beneath the waves, leaving nothing but a few pitiful islands of wreckage bobbing on the icy sea.

So *Glorious* died. The ten Gladiator pilots who had fought so gallantly against overwhelming odds, and who had flown that last patrol the day before, died with her.

One seeks a suitable epitaph for the brave Gladiators of

263 Squadron, and one seeks in vain. Bare figures alone must testify to their skill and courage. During the Norwegian Campaign, the Squadron lost only two Gladiators in air combat; but fifty enemy aircraft went flaming to destruction before their guns.

Relentlessly, the flames had crept across the Norwegian sky until they had consumed all resistance. When the shattered remnant of the Allied Expeditionary Force returned to Britain, there was no longer any doubt in anyone's mind.

The 'Phoney War' was over.

The *Blitzkrieg* had begun.

THE BRIDGES
AT MAASTRICHT

Too little – too late. That was the story of the RAF *in France during the dark days of May 1940, when the German Blitzkrieg swept all before it. This is the story of one mission, a brave and hopeless attack on the bridges over the Maas, which was to earn the* RAF *its first two Victoria Crosses of the war.*

SHORTLY BEFORE DAWN ON 11 MAY 1940, A LIGHT drizzle had fallen on Vraux Airfield, on the northern bank of the Aisne not far from Soissons. Already, as the sun rose over the Ardennes, its rays held the promise of heat; but at this early hour the air was fresh and cool, and diamonds of dew sparkled on the grass.

This morning, Vraux was the scene of unusual activity. On the flight-line, ground crews swarmed over the parked Blenheims of No. 114 Squadron, making last-minute checks. The aircraft were bombed-up and fuelled, ready to go. Take-off was in fifteen minutes. The aircrews had collected their parachutes and were lounging around on the grass, squinting into the rising sun, taking long drags at last cigarettes and discussing the latest news.

The Germans were on the move. After long months of relative quiet on the Western Front, their Panzer divisions had struck without warning, rumbling over the twisting roads of the Ardennes mountains and flooding out over the plains of Belgium and Luxembourg. Now, on this fine May morning, their armour was pouring over the Albert Canal and the Allied ground forces were screaming for air support. Today's target was the enemy build-up at Maastricht. Air Marshal Sir Arthur Barratt, Commander of the British Air Forces in France, was throwing all his resources into the battle. God knew, those resources were pitifully small. A few squadrons of Blenheims and outdated Fairey Battles, with a slender screen of Hurricanes, against the whole might of the Luftwaffe.

Time to go. Cigarette butts were thrown down and stamped out and the crews made for their aircraft.

At that moment, nine elongated shapes skipped over a line of trees and fanned out low across the airfield, furrowing the grass with their slipstream. For an instant men stood frozen, staring. Then they scattered in all directions, flinging themselves down, faces pressed against the sweet-smelling earth.

The world dissolved in a crescendo of sound as the Dornier 17s howled overhead, bomb-doors open. Showers of 100-pound bombs cascaded down and exploded among the Blenheims. The earth trembled. The snarl of engines faded away as the raiders pulled round in a screaming turn and vanished in the direction of the Aisne. Belatedly, a Vickers gun chattered.

The flight-lines was a shambles. Bodies of airmen sprawled among the shattered wreckage of the Blenheims. Oily black smoke climbed skywards from the lakes of blazing fuel. Minds dazed with shock, the survivors stared dumbly at the carnage, oblivious to the crackle of exploding ammunition.

In precisely forty-five seconds, No. 114 Squadron had ceased to exist.

Everywhere it was the same story. The Squadrons which were not caught napping on the ground were flung into the attack and decimated by the hordes of prowling Messerschmitts, and by the flak. It was thickest around the most important objective of all – the bridges at Maastricht, where every few yards along the banks of the river the long-barrelled 37-mm and the quadruple 20-mm cannon reared their ugly snouts. Across these bridges a continual stream of tanks, armoured cars and troop-carriers rumbled their way into Flanders.

On the morning of 12 May, Whit Sunday, nine Fairey Battles of the Belgian Air Force attacked the bridges through a wall of fire. Six Battles crashed in flames. The bridges still stood. A short while later the nine Blenheims of No. 139 Squadron had a try. They were caught by fifty Messerschmitt 109Es and massacred. Only one air-craft, its wings and fuselage riddled with bullet-holes, managed to escape.

Both these attacks had been made from high level. Air Marshal Barratt resolved to make the next attack a low-level strike. This might – just might – give the crews time to bomb and get clear before the full fury of the enemy defences burst upon them.

One hundred and twenty miles from Maastricht, near Reims, lay the little grass airfield of Amifontaine. Here were based the Fairey Battles of No. 12 Squadron, RAF. At eight o'clock on this lovely Whit Sunday morning, the crews of No. 12 – thirty young men in all – were crammed into the small operations hut listening in silence as the deputy CO, Squadron Leader Lowe, told them that six aircraft were to take off and attack the two bridges at Maastricht. Lowe paused, then said: 'This is going to be a job for volunteers. Will anyone who doesn't want to go please step forward?'

Not a man moved. Lowe, conscious of the fact that the crews detailed for the raid might not return, was faced with a terrible decision. Finally, he settled for the six crews already on standby. Three Battles would attack the bridge at Veldwezelt, and three the bridge at Vroen-hoven. The former was the task of 'B' Flight, led by twenty-two-year-old Flying Officer Donald ('Judy') Gar-land. Garland's opposite number in 'A' Flight was Flying Officer Norman Thomas, who would lead the attack on the Vroenhoven bridge.

Thomas was the first to take off, followed by Pilot

Officer Davy. The third member of 'A' Flight, Pilot Officer Brereton, had mechanical trouble with his aircraft and had to be left behind. Five minutes later, Garland's Battle bumped across the grass and roared into the air. Behind Garland came Flying Officer McIntosh and Sergeant Fred Marland.

Thomas and Davy climbed steadily at 160 mph, levelling off at 7000 feet. Scattered cloud was creeping across the sky from the east. Thomas glanced at his watch: nine o'clock. Tongeren was dead ahead. Fifteen miles further on lay Maastricht. Suddenly, black blotches of flak began to stain the sky around the two Battles. So the Germans had advanced this far already! Thomas and Davy came down to 5000 feet and altered course north-east, heading straight for the target.

Five minutes ahead of the Battles, the eight Hurricanes of No. 1 Fighter Squadron, based at Vassincourt, were streaking towards Maastricht. From the cockpit of the leading aircraft, Squadron Leader 'Bull' Halahan scanned the sky over the canal. High up, an aircraft's wing flashed silver in the sunlight. As Halahan watched, a whole swarm of tiny, glittering crosses slid into view. Ten, twenty, thirty, forty . . . Halahan stopped counting.

Climbing flat out, the Hurricanes sped towards the enemy. Those tiny silver crosses were the massed Messerschmitt 109s of *Jagdgeschwader* 1, 21 and 27, more than 120 fighters.

Guns hammering, the eight Hurricanes raced into the attack. It was hopeless. A hail of *Mauser* tore Halahan's plane in half and he bailed out just in time. Five more Hurricanes and three 109s crashed on the banks of the canal.

Under cover of the diversion, Thomas roared over the Maastricht–Tongeren road towards his objective, the concrete bridge at Vroenhoven. Suddenly the voice of his

gunner, Sergeant Campion, crackled over the intercom.
'Enemy fighter closing in starboard.'

'All right. Watch him.' Determinedly, Thomas held his
course. The Me. 109 turned and sped after Davy, who
dived into a cloud.

The flak was coming up thick and fast now, exploding
all around with a horrible, gritty crunch. Pearly tracers
arced lazily up, then streaked past viciously or smacked
through wings and fuselage. Thomas pointed the Battle's
nose at the bridge ahead and pushed forward the control
column. The needle of the altimeter unwound with
frightening speed . . . 4000 . . . 3500 . . . 3000 feet. Now!
Thomas pressed the bomb-release and one of his 250-
pounders dropped away, followed by the other three, singly.
The 'g' pressed him down into his seat as he hauled
back on the stick. The Battle groaned out of its screaming
dive and streaked across the canal at less than 100 feet,
running the gauntlet as the German gunners below poured
solid streams of shells after the fleeing aircraft. The Battle
shuddered again and again as shells ripped into it. Thomas
skipped over a German convoy which was blazing away
with everything it had. Then the engine spluttered and
died, Thomas wrestled desperately with the controls as
the Battle slewed to starboard. The aircraft smacked
down on its belly, bounced a couple of times and slid to a
stop. Dazed, but unhurt, the crew undid their straps and
climbed out of the cockpit. A burst of machine-gun fire
snickered above their heads. Men in field-grey uniforms
were running towards them across the field. Slowly, they
raised their hands.

Diving behind his leader, having managed to shake off
the 109, Pilot Officer Davy saw Thomas's bombs erupt on
the far end of the bridge. He dropped his own bombs
from 2000 feet and, to his disappointment, saw them explode in the water and on the canal bank. A string of flak

splashed across the sky ahead, so close that the Battle bucked on the shock-waves. Time to get out of it. Davy turned away and pushed the nose down, racing for home. At that moment he was attacked by a prowling 109. Davy's rear gunner damaged the fighter and drove it off, but not before cannon-shells had set fire to the port petrol tank. She might blow up at any second. Davy ordered his crew to bail out, and was about to follow them over the side when he noticed that the fire had gone out of its own accord. He nursed the crippled Battle towards base, and was only a few miles away from home when he ran out of fuel and had to come down in a field. A few hours later Mansell, Davy's observer, arrived back at Amifontaine. Patterson, the rear gunner, had not been so lucky. He came down behind the German lines and spent the rest of the war in a POW camp.

The bridge at Vroenhoven still stood. Five minutes after Thomas's attack, Garland's flight was approaching its metal twin at Veldwezelt. Garland favoured a low-level attack, and the three Battles swept across the Belgian landscape at fifty feet. In line astern, they plunged into a writhing cloud of flak bursts and a glare of darting tracers. Flying Officer McIntosh's aircraft was caught in a web of steel and erupted into flames. Despite terrible burns, McIntosh jettisoned his bombs and made a perfect belly-landing on the left bank of the canal. All three crew members scrambled out of the wreck and were taken prisoner.

A Battle staggered out of the smoke, burning from wingtip to wingtip and dragging an oily black banner in its wake. It was Fred Marland's aircraft. Suddenly, the nose went up and the Battle climbed steeply. For an agonizing moment it hung there, clawing the air with its propeller. Then it flicked over and dived vertically into the ground in a mushroom of smoke and flame. Not a hope of the crew bailing out.

The third Battle – Garland's – suddenly appeared over the bridge, turning steeply. Pieces fell from it as the sweating Wehrmacht gunners pumped hundreds of shells at it through red-hot barrels. Leaving a thin trail of smoke, the Battle plummeted at the target in a dive. The gunners ducked as a shattering explosion flung a column of spray skywards. A piece of wing, stamped with an RAF roundel, turned over and over in the air and splashed into the canal.

When the smoke cleared, the western end of the bridge was a tangled ruin, sagging into the water. The fields around the bridges were strewn with the burning wrecks of aircraft. Tall columns of smoke drifted slowly on the breeze. Already the German engineers were in action, throwing pontoons across the canal alongside the damaged Veldwezelt bridge. Relentlessly, the advance went on. The sacrifice had been in vain.

Garland and his observer, Sergeant Tom Gray, were posthumously awarded the Victoria Cross. They were the first RAF personnel to receive this award during the Second World War. Few people today remember the name of Garland's gunner, L.A.C. Reynolds, for he received no award at all.

DOUBLE SURVIVOR

It is a grim fact that, in time of war, at least one aircraft is destroyed accidentally for every machine lost on operations. This is the story of one such accident – and the courage of a badly injured survivor, struggling to bring help to a dying comrade.

SERGEANT JOSEF FUSNIAK WAS FEELING FAR FROM happy. It was bitterly cold in the rear-gun turret of the Wellington bomber, and to make matters worse he was nursing a mass of bruises down his right side, the result of a bad fall from his bicycle while on his way to briefing earlier that morning.

It was Saturday, 31 January 1942, an icy overcast winter's day with freezing temperatures and the promise of heavy snowfalls over most of the British Isles. It was not a good day for flying, but nineteen-year-old Fusniak and the five other members of his crew – all Polish like himself – were nearing the end of their course at the RAF operational training unit at Bramcote in Warwickshire and today's sortie, a routine cross-country navigation training flight, would bring them just that much nearer to flying with an operational squadron. That was the day they were all waiting for. The day when they could strike a blow against Nazi Germany. A blow for their own enslaved country.

As the Wellington taxied around the perimeter track Fusniak listened idly to the voices of the pilot and co-pilot, Flight Lieutenant Kujawa and Sergeant Polczyk, over the intercom, reading through the pre-flight checks. Minutes later the twin-engined bomber was thundering down the runway and lifting into the grey freezing sky.

The Wellington climbed steadily northwards, the intercom crackling busily with instructions about course, height and throttle settings, all the technical jargon-laden chatter that is second nature to bomber crews. Fusniak, in his remote rear turret, busied himself checking the twin Browning .303 machine guns, ensuring that they were moving freely and that the hydraulics which trained his turret were working. Unless they encountered a marauding German fighter – and that was unlikely in weather like this – there would be little for him to do but sit there and keep as warm as he could. He shivered slightly as a few snowflakes drifted past his turret and settled himself more snugly into the fur-lined folds of his leather flying jacket. The Wellington droned on over the featureless snow-covered landscape. To pass the time he tried to identify the landmarks which the navigator, Flying Officer Bieganski, told the crew to look out for. At about ten minutes past twelve he looked down and saw a sizeable town nestling among hills and valleys. According to Bieganski that would be Skipton.

The next instant the whole scene was blotted out by a wall of opaque whiteness that swept past the Wellington. In an instant, as it flew into the heart of the blizzard, the great bomber became like a blind bird helplessly groping its way towards clear sky. All the pilots could do was keep a steady course and trust their instruments.

Disaster struck without warning at precisely twelve-fifteen. There was a terrific crash and Fusniak was slammed brutally against the steel doors that led from his turret into the rear fuselage. He was conscious of a terrific crack on the head, of a terrible pain in his left leg, of being tossed about the interior of the gun turret like some helpless puppet. Then there was nothing but a buzzing in his ears and a strange grey drifting sensation that turned into blackness.

His first impression as he struggled back to consciousness was of a low moaning noise that sounded like a soul in torment. After long seconds he realized that it was the wail of the wind. Painfully he turned his head and looked around him. The blizzard still raged and everything was still obscured by a white veil. He knew that something had happened, but his numbed brain could not grasp what it was. He fumbled behind his back for the turret door catch, intending to enter the fuselage. The next instant he overbalanced and fell out of the turret into a pile of wet snow. It was only then that he realized that the Wellington had crashed.

As he floundered in the snowdrift a stabbing pain shot through his left leg, forcing a cry of agony from his lips. His fingers explored the course of the pain and came into contact with a sharp object, the broken end of a bone. The waves of pain ebbed slowly. He sat nursing his leg and looked around. In front of him the turret lay like an island in the snow. A few yards away there was a jumble of stone, the wreckage of the wall that had torn the Wellington brutally from the sky. Only three feet more altitude and she would have flown on, the crew unaware of their hairsbreadth escape from danger.

Slowly Fusniak became aware of the terrible cold slicing through his flying clothing like a knife. Snowflakes swept across the frozen ground like bullets, driven by the howling north-east wind. The icy particles tore at his face and hands, opening up areas of raw pain. He knew that he had to move or die.

Trailing his shattered left leg behind him he began to crawl, searching for the wreck of the aircraft. A few minutes later, through the swirling snowflakes, he made out the dark bulk of the fuselage and inched his way towards it. The fuselage was little more than a twisted metal tube; the wings had gone and so had nose and tail.

He crawled along the metal length searching for some sign of life. As he rounded the area of torn metal where the nose had been he picked out five dark bundles lying in a semi-circle in the snow. Sobbing, he clawed his way towards them.

The first one he reached was Flight Lieutenant Kujawa. He was obviously dead. So was the second pilot, Sergeant Polczyk. Fusniak crawled on to the next body, that of Flying Officer Bieganski, the navigator. He too was dead. A few yards away lay the front gunner, Sergeant Tokarzewski. There was no life in his broken body either. Only the wireless operator, Sergeant Sadowski, had survived the terrible impact. He was alive, but only just. Blood was already staining the snow beneath his body. Fusniak realized that had it not been for his rearwards facing position in the gun turret, which had helped to cushion the brutal deceleration from 200 mph to a standstill within yards, his own shattered body would have been lying there in the snow with his comrades.

He realized something else, too. He had to get help, and quickly. Not just for himself but for Sadowski. The wireless operator was terribly hurt; perhaps he was already dying. But if Fusniak could get help soon enough then there might just be a chance of saving his life. He crawled back to the Wellington's broken fuselage and searched for the first aid kit. It was not there. His search yielded only three tins of tomato soup and a parachute pack. Stuffing the cans inside his flying jacket, he dragged the parachute pack to where Sadowski lay. He pulled the rip cord and caught the folds of silk that billowed out, spreading them over Sadowski's body, pressing them round it like a cocoon. A piece of wreckage propped upright in the snow would give the wounded man some shelter from the terrible wind.

Fusniak tried to make the man understand that he was

going for help, but there was no sign that he had heard, not even a flicker of recognition on the drawn, pain-racked face. Tearing a strip of wood from the fuselage to use as a makeshift crutch, Fusniak took one last look at his friend and then dragged himself upright, taking the first tentative step on his long journey towards civilization. The next instant his crutch snapped in half, flinging him headlong in the snow. The bone in his leg grated savagely and for some time he was unable to move. Then, as the red mist of pain cleared, he used the remaining two-foot length of wood like a punt pole, dragging himself through the snow. He had no way of knowing where he was. All he knew was that he had to head downhill.

In fact the Wellington had crashed on the top of Buckden Pike, a 2,302-foot peak overlooking Yorkshire's Wharfedale. Although only fifty miles north of the industrial heart of Yorkshire, Buckden Pike lay in country as bleak and wild as any in the British Isles. It was barren enough in mid-summer, but in a January blizzard it was deadly. Fusniak went on crawling painfully, keeping the wind in his face. That was his first mistake, for the wind was coming from the north-east and he was heading in the wrong direction. Ahead of him lay only the wastes of Walden Moor, mile upon mile of rolling hills scarred by crags and cruel ravines. He could travel for miles before striking a road or a village, and long before that happened Josef Fusniak would be dead.

He had gone a long way down the slopes of the pike before some sixth sense told him that he had gone wrong. Somehow he knew that he had to turn around, claw his way up the pike again and start afresh. A couple of feet at a time, the pain from his leg jarring through his body, he began to drag himself uphill once more. Mercifully, the fury of the blizzard had abated somewhat and he was able to see some of his surroundings. The slope began to level out again and he stopped to get his breath. Despite the awful cold he was bathed in sweat. Desperately, he prayed harder than he had ever prayed before. Prayed for some sign to show him the right way to take.

Then the miracle happened. A few feet in front of his eyes he saw a double line of paw prints leading away through the snow. His numbed mind searched back to his days as a boy scout back in Poland, where he had studied animals and their ways. What he was looking at was the trail of a fox. Frantically, he groped for it – and then it came to him in a flash.

In winter foxes moved down from the hills and slunk up to farms in their desperate search for food.

There was no time to lose. At any moment the frail track might be obliterated by a fresh snowstorm. His lungs bursting with exertion, his hands frozen and swollen like balloons as they grasped his stick, he dragged himself along the trail, his only life-line in that awful sea of white.

It was a nightmare, a petrified wilderness that seemed to stretch on for eternity. He clawed his way on, uphill, downhill, slithering over banked-up drifts against stone walls with nothing to hear but the sobbing of his own breath and the dreadful scream of the wind. Foot after foot, yard after yard, for more than four miles, torn apart by agony, Josef Fusniak forced himself on.

He was almost blind with exhaustion now. The trail of paw prints swam in front of his eyes. Then, abruptly, terrifyingly, they disappeared. Frantically he looked around and saw that the paw prints had swung off to the right. Peering ahead he saw why. A few feet away the ground vanished. Beyond was a void of swirling snow, a sheer drop down a rock face to the floor of a quarry far below.

The track headed downhill once more. It was growing fainter now and Fusniak knew that if he lost it he too would be lost. Only that tenuous track gave him the will to go on. The knowledge that somewhere in this awful wilderness there was another living creature.

He was in a valley now, wallowing in deep snow. He willed himself to go on faster, ignoring the pain in his leg. Then, abruptly, the fox's trail disappeared. Weeping, Fusniak looked up. A few yards in front of him was a wall. He floundered towards it, reaching for its top with frozen hands. He pulled himself up, but his weakened arms relaxed and he collapsed in a heap at its foot again. He tried again and failed. The wall was only four feet high, but for Fusniak in his exhausted state it was too much.

As he lay there in the shelter of the wall a strange peace floated over him. He was sleepy. If only he could rest there for a few minutes, dozing and regaining his strength, he would be all right. The drowsiness crept up from his legs. He was warm now, and the pain had gone. His eyelids closed and he did not want to open them again. Josef Fusniak was dying from exposure.

Suddenly he remembered his parents, his childhood in Warsaw, his school, joining the Polish Air Force, his training, first as a pilot then as an air-gunner. Everything flashed through his mind. He began to cry because he remembered that up in the hills his friend was lying terribly injured, waiting for his help, and now he could not help him. His eyes were full of tears. He began praying again, praying that the awful drowsiness would leave him, that somehow he would find the strength to move.

He opened his eyes again and saw the most remarkable thing of his life. Up to that moment the whole world had been white and grey – white snow and grey clouds. Then, suddenly a gap appeared in the overcast sky and a brilliant ray of sunshine slanted down to light up the hillside some distance away. To Josef Fusniak, a deeply religious boy, it was as though heaven had sent him a sign, an encouragement to carry on. New strength flooded through his body. Once again he reached up, seized the top of the wall, pulled his body up and flopped over. He rolled down a slope on the other side, shouting for help at the top of his voice, and came to a stop at the bank of a stream.

At that moment, through the mist that once again threatened to obscure his eyes, he saw two figures running towards him.

It was four-thirty, three hours and fifteen minutes since Fusniak had tumbled from his gun turret on the barren heights of Buckden Pike.

The men who stumbled on the exhausted Fusniak – William Parker, licensee of the White Lion Hotel in the nearby village of Cray, and his brother – thought at first that the injured airman was a German. Nevertheless, they lifted him as gently as possible and carried him to the hotel where Parker settled him down in front of a roaring fire and forced a glass of whisky down his throat. Frantically, in his broken English, Fusniak tried to make them understand that there was another injured man on top of the pike. He was desperately anxious in case the Parkers had not grasped his meaning. But he need not have worried. William Parker was already on his way, ploughing through the snowdrifts towards the village of Buckden, two miles away, where there was a telephone.

As soon as he heard the news of the crashed aircraft, Buckden's village policeman, Jack Galloway, made a gallant attempt to reach the wreck, but by this time the blizzard was howling with renewed ferocity and he was driven back. A truckload of soldiers was also sent out from a nearby army camp but they too were defeated by the weather. So were a local farmer and five other men who tackled the pike roped together for safety.

It was not until two o'clock the following morning that

a local landowner, Mr Close, battled his way through on horseback to the shattered remains of the Wellington. He was too late. Sadowski was dead, a pathetic bundle lying under the silk of his parachute and a shroud of snow. Josef Fusniak, by now unconscious and unaware of his friend's death, was taken to hospital in Skipton, twenty-two miles away. It was not until several days later that someone broke the news to him that the wireless operator had died on the hillside along with the others.

Fusniak stayed in Skipton for six weeks, first in hospital and then as the guest of a family who befriended him and brought him chocolate and cigarettes. He made a full recovery and returned to the RAF to complete his training. Soon afterwards he received the British Empire Medal in recognition of his gallant journey to try and save his comrade. It was the first BEM to be awarded to a Polish airman.

On 22 July 1942, Fusniak, now a member of No. 301 Squadron, took off from RAF Hemswell near Lincoln for a bombing raid on Duisburg. Over the target his Wellington was coned by searchlights and crippled by heavy anti-aircraft fire. The bomber exploded and Fusniak was flung clear. He descended safely by parachute into a captivity which ended when the United States Army liberated him in April 1945. For a second time he had survived when every other member of his crew had died.

Fusniak married after the war and settled in Kent. Every year he travels to Yorkshire, visiting the people who were so kind to him after his ordeal and making the pilgrimage to the top of Buckden Pike. There, one year, he erected a cross from the wreckage on the spot where the Wellington had smashed herself to pieces. It is nine feet tall and mounted on a cairn of stone, and on a polished marble tablet are carved the words 'Thanksgiving to God, the Parker family and local people, and in memory of five

Polish RAF airmen who died here on 31.1.1942, buried in Newark. The survivor.' And there is something else too, a reminder of the miracle that saved Josef Fusniak's life. Cemented into the cairn is a tiny figurine of a fox.

ORDEAL IN THE FOREST

The war on the Eastern Front, 1941–5, was characterized by unparalleled savagery – and unparalleled acts of courage on both sides. This chapter tells of courage and fortitude of a kind that must surely stand alone in the story of human endurance ; the iron determination of a man to survive appalling injuries and conditions and to fight again.

CONSCIOUSNESS RETURNED SLOWLY AND RELUCT-antly to Lieutenant Alexei Maressyev. With it came pain: waves of searing agony that engulfed his legs and stabbed through his numbed brain like red-hot needles. He was lying in deep snow in the middle of a pine forest. At first, he could not recall what he was doing there. He could only think of his legs, crumpled under him at an unnatural angle. He tried to sit up, and the agony became unbearable. Merciful blackness enveloped him and he fell back in the snow once more.

It had been a routine mission. On that April morning in 1942, Maressyev's squadron of Soviet Air Force Yak-1 fighters had been detailed to escort a formation of Russian bombers in an attack on the German-occupied airfield of Staraya Russa, in the Ukraine. The mission had been a success; the bombers had attacked their objectives and Maressyev had shot down two lumbering Junkers 52 transports that had tried to take off while the raid was in progress.

Then the German fighters had pounced, and the Russian aircraft had found themselves in the middle of a twisting dogfight with Messerschmitt 109s. Seconds later, Maressyev's fighter shuddered as cannon shells slammed into it. Its controls shot away, the Yak plummeted earth-wards. There had been no time for Maressyev to bale out.

59

His last memory was of the forest, whirling up to meet him, before the aircraft hit the treetops and broke up, hurling him from the cockpit.

It was hours before he came to his senses again, the pain in his legs numbed now by the freezing cold. Suddenly, a rustling sound in the trees behind him jerked him fully awake. He turned his head painfully in the direction of the noise, and froze in horror. An enormous bear was shambling towards him, its yellow eyes boring into him. The creature stopped short a few yards away and reared menacingly on its hind legs.

Frantically, Maressyev groped for his service revolver. He had no idea whether it would still work, but it was his only chance. His hands trembled violently as he fought to hold the weapon steady. The explosion was deafening in the stillness of the forest. The bear staggered, then subsided to the ground in a twitching mountain of fur. The pilot's aim had been good.

Shivering with reaction, Maressyev took stock of his situation. An examination of his legs revealed that both were broken and crushed below the knees. He dare not take off his flying boots, for he knew that he would never be able to get them on again, and without them frostbite would set in rapidly.

The dogfight with the Messerschmitts had carried him a long way inside enemy territory, and he had no way of knowing how far he was from the Russian lines. Dimly, he could hear the rumble of guns; they might be fifty or a hundred miles away. He knew only that he had to keep moving towards them, towards the east. He was twenty-six years old and at the peak of his strength, and in his heart there was the grim determination that somehow he would win through.

He made a makeshift crutch from a fallen branch and dragged himself upright. The pain from his shattered legs almost made him faint again, but he fought against the searing agony and began to pull himself laboriously, foot by foot, on the first stage of his journey. Hour after hour, day after day, he forced himself to go on, falling every few yards and lying there in the snow until his strength returned. At night he crawled into the undergrowth and spent the hours of darkness dozing fitfully, awakened frequently by the bitter cold and spasms of pain.

Day after day, the long agony went on. He no longer had the strength to remain upright, and was forced to drag himself through the snow on all fours, like a wounded animal. On the seventh day he found some food – a handful of hard berries which he crammed into his mouth and ate ravenously. Later, he stumbled on the body of an ss trooper, with a dagger lying beside it. He used the weapon to kill a hedgehog, which he tore apart and ate raw. After that, he existed on handfuls of ants, which he scooped up, crushed into a paste and devoured greedily.

His youth, and the intermittent rumble of guns in the east, kept him going. He had lost all sense of time now; day and night merged into a continuous greyness, and only the occasional tearing stab of pain from his legs forced him back to reality.

On the nineteenth day he heard the voices of children. He lay on his face in the undergrowth, willing his sobbing breath to be still so that he could hear better, praying that it was not an hallucination. But his imagination was not playing tricks; some time later, partisans came upon his emaciated body lying senseless by the side of a forest trail. They lifted him gently and carried him back to their hideout, a series of underground caves. It was three days before Maressyev could tell them who he was. Once they learned his identity, they quickly got a message to the nearest Soviet airfield via their efficient communication system. Within hours, a little Po-2 ambulance aircraft was on its way to a secret forest airstrip. The next day, after emergency treatment, the injured pilot was flown to a military hospital near Moscow.

When he came round after a lengthy operation, Maressyev knew that he no longer had any feet. He had known all along that the surgeons would have to amputate, once gangrene had set in. As the days went by, he sank deeper into black despair. He would never fly again. He was an invalid, a ruined man. Thanks to his constitution, he suffered no ill-effects from his amputations, but he lost the will to live. Helplessly, the doctors and nurses watched him slowly wasting away.

It was a Red Army colonel in the next bed who saved his life. One day, the officer handed over a magazine; in it was the story of a Russian fighter pilot of the First World War, Karpovich, who had been shot down and lost a leg. Despite everything, he had refused to give in. He had been fitted with an artificial limb and had continued to fly and fight.

The story, and the cheerful encouragement of the colonel, himself an amputee, gave Maressyev new hope. From that day on, he had one goal: to get back into the air as a fighter pilot. He began to sleep soundly again, and little by little his appetite came back, so that before long he was being issued with double rations. He began a strict programme of physical exercises, designed to bring back strength to his wasted muscles.

His stumps healed rapidly, and at last the great day came when he was fitted with artificial feet. The doctors told him that he would have to learn to walk all over again, first of all with the aid of crutches and then with a stick. Half jokingly, they assured him that eventually he would be able to ride a bicycle, dance the polka and even fly again. But Maressyev was not joking; he was determined to achieve all those things.

He devised new exercises to add to the set programme. Twice a day he would go for a walk along the corridor, gradually increasing the distance until he was able to cover the fifty yards forty-five times without tiring himself too much. Already he was achieving something, for this was the distance that usually separated the operations room from dispersal on a front-line fighter airfield. At other times, he would sit in his chair and spend hours going through all the leg movements required of a pilot.

From the hospital, Maressyev went for a period of convalescence to a special sanatorium for aircrew on the outskirts of Moscow. On the day after his arrival some of the other patients were treated to a strange sight. Before breakfast, Maressyev came into the garden wearing only his pyjama trousers. He looked around and, satisfied that no one was watching, or so he thought, he began to run in short, jerky bounds, his elbows held tightly to his sides. After a couple of hundred yards he suddenly collapsed, gasping for breath and covered in sweat. He lay immobile for a few minutes, then got up and began to run again. He was almost exhausted, but still he forced himself to go on, his face twisted with pain. Another item of news, even more surprising, went the rounds of the sanatorium. The footless pilot, it seemed, was crazy about dancing. Having learned that the sanatorium's pretty young secretary liked nothing better than to dance, it had been quite easy for Maressyev to persuade her to give him some lessons. It was harder for him than it seemed.

In the evening, dancing was the favourite pastime of the convalescents. Maressyev soon became an outstanding figure at each gathering, never missing a dance. His cheeks burning, his eyes shining with the effort, he would carefully follow every movement with an ease that amazed his friends. None suspected what it cost him, or the reason for his periodic disappearances from the dance floor.

As soon as he stepped into the shadows, the smile on his face would turn to a grimace of pain. Clutching the balustrade he would stagger down the flight of steps to throw himself full length on the grass, his body racked by sobs of agony, driven from him by his tortured stumps. He would loosen the straps of his artificial feet a little, to ease the pain. Then, after a few minutes, he would get up and return to the dance floor as though nothing had happened.

His convalescence over, Maressyev was ordered to appear before an Air Ministry board for reclassification. He passed the medical examination easily, and when the members of the board hesitated over the question of his feet he offered to demonstrate his ability by dancing. He performed so well that the board classified him 'Fit for flying duties after an appropriate refresher course'.

Maressyev left the boardroom with a light heart. There seemed to be no obstacles in his way back to a flying career. However, it was not to prove as simple as he thought. Even at the height of the war, with the Air Force crying out for reserves of aircrew, the regulations still remained hard and fast. Not only were candidates required to have a perfect physique and iron nerves, but the least infirmity such as the loss of a finger or a toe was sufficient to prevent acceptance. As for a man who expected to fly a sensitive, high-powered fighter without feet, the idea was preposterous.

Maressyev was summoned before a second board. He showed his documents, he pleaded, he argued, but it was no use. The regulations said that a man could not fly without any feet, and that was that. Nobody was going to bend the rules for the sake of a mere lieutenant.

In spite of everything, the board was sympathetic towards Maressyev. He was offered a ground job, or the choice of a transfer to another service. Maressyev stumped out, fuming with anger, and went looking for the presi-

dent of the first board, the one which had classified him
fit for flying. The president was very sympathetic. The
only thing he could do, he said, was to write a letter of
recommendation to the Air Officer Commanding *Istrebi-
telnya Aviatsiya* (Fighter Command), who could probably
find Maressyev a ground post directly involved with
operations. Maressyev shook his head. It was flying, or
nothing.

There was only one course of action left open to him.
He decided to take his case directly to the c-in-c, General
of the Air Force Alexander A. Novikov, a veteran air ace
who was greatly respected throughout the service. He, if
anyone, would understand Maressyev's predicament, and
only he would have the power to make the necessary
breach in the brick wall of the regulations.

Maressyev's visit to Novikov was brief, and it was an
unqualified success. He came away with a note in his
pocket which read: 'Lieutenant A. Maressyev has been
interviewed by the Commander-in-Chief. It is the latter's
wish that this officer be given all possible assistance to
enable him to return to flying duties with Fighter Command.'

After that, it was ridiculously easy. Within a week,
Maressyev was on his way to a flying training school.

He had won one victory, but the next battle was still to
come. Only time would tell if he was capable of standing
up to the renewed strain of handling a fighter in combat.

The pupils of the flying school to which Maressyev was
posted were all ex-hospital cases, and at this stage of the
war the school was packed to capacity. The commanding
officer, a very harassed individual, sent Maressyev off to
a vacancy in a flight without even bothering to look at his
papers. The pilot spent the first day settling in, quickly
readjusting to the familiar atmosphere he had missed so
badly during the last months. He also took the oppor-

tunity of getting a shoemaker to fit small straps to his flying boots, so that his feet could be buckled firmly to the rudder pedals of his aircraft.

His first flight, the next morning, did much to restore his confidence. He felt quite at home in the cockpit of the little trainer. His expert touch was still there, and as the weeks went by he became complete master of his aircraft once more. He ended the course with an assessment that read: 'An excellent pilot, enthusiastic and keen. Fit for flying duties in any branch of the Air Force.'

Another hurdle had been overcome, but Maressyev still had to pass through an operational training unit to become familiar with the latest fighter types. The aircraft he had flown before his crash were now outdated and the factories were producing the more modern Yak-9 and La-5, aircraft which could compete on equal terms with the Luftwaffe's Messerschmitt 109Fs and Focke-Wulf 190s.

The new Lavochkin La-5 was lighter on the controls than any fighter Maressyev had handled. In fact it was too sensitive, too responsive to his touch for him to enjoy the 'feel' of flying it. His leg reactions were not quick enough during tight manoeuvres, and more than once he nearly caused the Lavochkin to flick into a spin. He found to his dismay that he lacked the essential quality of a good fighter pilot: perfect unity between himself and his machine.

For the first time since he was in hospital, Maressyev nearly gave up hope. Yet he persevered, critically analysing his technique as a pilot, examining every small detail. It became clear that he would have to develop a new set of reflexes, so that his stumps could transmit to his brain feelings which would normally be transmitted by the soles of his feet, or his toes. Gradually, his feverish efforts achieved some results, but still there was something missing. Just as he thought he had finally surmounted his difficulties something else would go wrong, throwing him almost back to square one.

Then, one day in March 1943, when the first warm wind of spring was melting the snow, Maressyev thundered down the runway in a spray of water, whirled up from the muddy pools. There was a crosswind blowing and take-off was not easy, as the La-5 kept drifting to port.

At the peak of his climb, Maressyev suddenly felt an almost-forgotten sensation. It took him a few moments to realize what it was. Then, in a flash, he knew. He was part of his aircraft again. Hardly daring to believe, he tried a steep turn to starboard. The fighter responded beautifully. He put the nose down in a shallow dive and opened the throttle. The big Shvetsov radial roared out its song of power, hurling him across the sky at 400 mph. Back with the stick and up to 15,000 feet, where, gently and lovingly, he put the Lavochkin through a series of slow rolls. He sang for sheer joy. A couple of loops, a flick roll for good measure, and he headed jubilantly for home, knowing for certain that he had tamed the thoroughbred at last.

Maressyev returned to the front in July 1943, after an absence of fifteen months. His new squadron was based on an airfield near Kursk, and he arrived just in time to take part in the great battle which was to begin a few days later. The Luftwaffe had been out in strength lately, and everyone knew that something big was developing. On the night of Maressyev's arrival, and for several nights more, the Germans bombed the airfield. Maressyev, who had already been machine-gunned by a stray Messerschmitt on his way there, crouched in a slit trench and felt miserable.

The battle began with a vicious, thundering artillery duel, followed by wave upon wave of bombers. The Ger-

mans quickly realized that their original plan – to surprise
the Russians by a pincer movement and encircle the
greater part of their army following a breakthrough to
north and south of Kursk – had failed. The Soviet High
Command waited until all enemy units were engaged,
then launched a counter-attack.

Maressyev's squadron was held in reserve, and it was
not until the second day that they were ordered to take
off. Their task was to provide fighter cover for the tanks
which were now rolling towards the German lines through
heavy artillery fire.

The battlefield was wreathed in smoke, and Maressyev
could see several T-34 tanks burning. Then his Squadron
Leader's voice crackled in his earphones: 'Stukas on the
left, below. Attack, Falcons, attack!'

There they were – twenty Junkers 87 dive-bombers,
flying serenely through the anti-aircraft bursts. The Russian
fighters manoeuvred until the sun was behind them, then,
in line astern, they ripped through the enemy formation.
A Junkers staggered drunkenly and fell away, one wing
wrapped in flames. Another spun down, leaving a twisting
spiral of black smoke.

Maressyev closed in on the tail of a Stuka. The distance
closed rapidly until he could see every detail of the enemy;
the mottled camouflage, with the white-edged black
crosses standing out on the wings and fuselage; the rear
gunner, crouching over his weapon. Maressyev pressed
the firing button and the long glasshouse cockpit flew to
pieces. There was a flicker of flame at the wing root, and
suddenly the Stuka was a ball of fire, turning over and
over.

He broke away and went after another Junkers. This
one was no novice; he twisted and turned in an effort to
shake off the determined Russian clinging to his tail. It
was no use. A long, hammering burst of cannon and

machine-gun fire, and it was all over. The Ju.87 went down and exploded in an oily mushroom of smoke.

Maressyev looked around to find himself alone in the sky. Away to the right, three columns of smoke rose towards the scattered clouds. Strangely enough, he felt no elation over his two victories. He had proved himself in battle, but it no longer seemed to matter. Wearily, he turned for home.

As the fighting on the ground raged with bestial savagery, the fighting in the air grew more intense. The next day, Maressyev's squadron was on patrol over the front when a shoal of blunt-nosed fighters slid by to starboard, at a lower altitude. They were Focke-Wulf 190s, the first Maressyev had seen. The Russians dived flat out towards the enemy, who so far had not seen them. Suddenly, the German fighters scattered in all directions. Maressyev hauled back on the stick and half-rolled off the top of a loop. A Lavochkin shot past with a 190 in hot pursuit. Just as the German was about to deliver the *coup de grâce* Maressyev got in a solid burst which tore off the 190's tail unit. He went down on his back and disappeared. Maressyev looked around and noticed another Focke-Wulf flying along straight and level, apparently unconcerned by the dogfights going on all over the sky. The German never knew what hit him. A long burst from Maressyev's guns and he went into a spin, wrapped in flames.

Maressyev turned steeply. A black dot in the centre of his windscreen grew rapidly larger: a 190, cannon winking, heading straight for him. Grimly, Maressyev levelled out and held the La-5 steady. Tracer flashed over his cockpit. One of them would have to break, or there would be a collision.

At the last instant, the German pulled up steeply and Maressyev ripped off a burst into his pale grey, oil-streaked belly. The Focke-Wulf fluttered down and exploded on the ground.

Guards Major Alexei Maressyev finished the war with a score of fifteen enemy aircraft destroyed. After the end of hostilities he took up a post in an Air Ministry department, retiring in 1949. He subsequently became a lecturer for the Academy of Social Sciences and toured the Soviet Union, speaking mainly to youth organizations. Today, he is head of the Soviet War Veterans' Association.

On his breast, in recognition of his courage and endurance, he wears the gold star of a Hero of the Soviet Union. He married soon after the war; a girl named Olga, who had fought in the Battle of Stalingrad and who herself had received the Order of the Red Star for gallantry. They live in Moscow and have one son, Victor.

COVER OF DARKNESS

The story of the Allied agents operating in the occupied countries, and the fearful risks they ran, is well known. What is not so well known is the story of the men who flew them to secret locations deep inside enemy territory, their only defence the cloak of darkness.

THE TWIN-ENGINED LOCKHEED HUDSON BOMBER shuddered and vibrated alarmingly as Flying Officer John Affleck held the throttles wide open. Outside the trembling fuselage the small group of passengers he was to take on board waited apprehensively, their faces showing pale through the darkness.

It was no use. The aircraft was stuck fast, its wheels bogged down in clinging mud. In a couple of hours' time it would be dawn, and with it would come discovery – and perhaps death. For this was 7 February 1944, and the Hudson was in a field near Dijon in German-occupied France.

John Affleck and his crew belonged to one of the most secret units in the wartime RAF, No. 161 (Special Duties) Squadron. Equipped mainly with twin-engined Hudsons and slow-flying Westland Lysanders, the squadron's task was to operate a kind of shuttle service across the channel, delivering agents and saboteurs to various locations in the occupied countries of Western Europe on behalf of clandestine Special Operations Executive. The pilots had no idea of the identity of the people they were carrying; the agents were known simply as 'Joes'. All operations were carried out at low level where map reading, particularly at night, was extremely difficult and required a great deal of skill on the part of the pilots. Navigation, however, was the least of the problems. As the months went by the German *Abwehr,* the Military Intelligence Service, made inroads into the ranks of the various resistance movements in occupied Europe and on several occasions aircraft were lost when, instead of resistance workers, they were greeted by heavily-armed Wehrmacht troops acting on information torn from members of the resistance who had broken down under torture.

Now, on this February night in 1944, it looked like the end for John Affleck, together with his crew and the group of hunted resistance members he was to have flown to safety. Among them was a young man who had been captured by the Germans and sentenced to death. Somehow his wife had managed to smuggle him out of the death cell, and now the whole family – mother, father and young daughter – were to be evacuated. To complicate matters even further the woman was pregnant and obviously very near her time.

Affleck shut down his engines, climbed from the cockpit and wearily explained the situation to the Frenchmen. Glancing at his watch, he told them that by his reckoning they had about ninety minutes in which to free the aircraft. If they had not got it clear of the mud at the end of that time they would have to set fire to it to prevent it falling into enemy hands. He warned them that he had already created enough racket to waken the dead, and with a German army garrison less than three miles away it was quite possible that enemy troops were already on their way to the landing ground.

All hands immediately set to work to try and push the aircraft clear, but it was hopeless. The Hudson was too heavy, and by this time its rear fuselage had sunk to ground level. Suddenly, everyone stiffened in apprehension as dark shapes came stealthily through the trees towards them. The scare, however, was soon over. The newcomers were inhabitants of a nearby village who had been alerted by the noise and had come to see what was going on. Affleck explained the situation to them and someone went off to fetch horses and oxen. These were quickly harnessed to the Hudson while the Frenchmen set to work with picks and shovels, digging trenches away from the wheels of the aircraft. After an hour their efforts were rewarded. The horses and oxen gave one last heave and the Hudson came free with a gigantic sucking noise.

Affleck lost no time in climbing aboard and restarting the engines. With his passengers safely inside he taxied cautiously round the field, then turned into the wind and gave the engines full throttle.

Halfway down the field he knew with blinding clarity that he was not going to make it. The Hudson's take-off speed was 90 knots, and with the trees at the far side rushing closer the airspeed indicator showed only 50 knots. Then the miracle happened. The Hudson hit a bump and lurched into the air. Somehow it kept flying, teetering on the edge of the stall while Affleck took it over the tree-tops with only feet to spare.

Shortly after daybreak, the Hudson touched down at Tempsford, No. 161 Squadron's base. While Affleck and his exhausted crew tumbled into their beds an ambulance whisked the Frenchwoman off to hospital. There, a few hours later, she gave birth to a daughter.

The kind of hair-raising experience that confronted Affleck was by no means uncommon among the pilots of 161 Squadron. Although Lockheed Hudsons were used whenever a large load of passengers had to be carried, in many respects they were far from ideal aircraft for operation from the rudimentary French landing grounds, which were often of a marshy nature, and it was the single-engined Lysander which bore the brunt of 161's dangerous work. The Lysanders flown by 161 Squadron were specially modified for their Special Duties' task. A 150-gallon auxiliary fuel tank was fitted between the undercarriage struts to give added range and a metal ladder was attached to the fuselage near the rear cockpit to help speed up the disembarking and embarking of agents on the Continent. One passenger was the usual load on the outward trip because of the weight of fuel carried, but on the return journey the Lysander, originally designed as a two-seater aircraft would carry up to four passengers in addition to the pilot. As underground activity on the Continent increased, however, it was found that even four agents on one trip were not always sufficient – hence the use of the Hudsons. If the landing field was too small for the larger aircraft, the mission was carried out by two or three Lysanders flying to the objective via different routes and making rendezvous at the same time over the landing ground.

On average, the special pick-up aircraft spent less than three minutes on the ground at their destinations in occupied territory. The rule was to get into the secret landing strips and out again as quickly as possible. Occasionally, however, unforseen circumstances caused lengthy delays and the rule had to be broken.

On the night of 26 January 1943, for example, a Lysander flown by Wing Commander Percy Pickard – who had just taken over as CO of 161 Squadron and who was later to lose his life in the daring low-level attack on Amiens Prison – circled over a secret rendezvous in France for no less than one and three-quarter hours before a flashing light from the ground gave him the all-clear to land. He dropped the agent he was carrying and picked up two others, heading for home by the shortest possible route. When he landed at an airstrip in Cornwall in the early hours of the morning his fuel gauges were reading empty.

Sometimes the Lysander pilots had to contend with unforseen obstacles as they groped their way down through the darkness towards the pinpoints of light that denoted their landing grounds. One pilot, Flight Lieutenant Bridger, misjudged his landing and opened the throttle to go round again – and flew straight into a power cable stretched across the far end of the field. The darkness dissolved in a vivid blue-white flash, but although he was temporarily blinded Bridger managed to keep the aircraft flying. Circling round the field, he made another approach and this time brought the aircraft in for what should have been a perfect landing. What he did not know, however, was that one of his tyres had burst when he hit the cable and the machine swung wildly before he managed to bring it to a stop.

Bridger disembarked his agent, took another one on board for the return trip then wondered what to do. With a burst tyre it would be almost impossible to get the Lysander out of the field, which was uneven. After a few moments thought he did the only thing possible; he took out his service revolver and put a bullet through the Lysander's good tyre. With the aircraft's equilibrium restored, albeit somewhat shakily, he managed to make a reasonable take-off, dodging the cables and heading out into the night towards England.

Sometimes, pilots found that the landing grounds they had been allocated were in the hands of the enemy. It happened to veteran Lysander pilot Squadron Leader A. M. Murphy, who encountered a hot reception when he brought his machine in to land at a site near Neufchateau on the night of 9 December 1941. Unknown to Murphy the reception committee that awaited him consisted not of resistance workers but of heavily-armed German troops who had surrounded the field. As the Lysander touched down a machine-gun chattered and a bullet struck Murphy in the neck. Streaming blood he pushed open the throttle, sending the Lysander bouncing over the uneven ground. Turning steeply to avoid a line of trees he headed away from the scene at low level, and although weak from loss of blood he managed to bring his bullet-riddled machine safely home.

Because of the low altitude at which the Lysanders flew there was little interference from enemy night-fighters. On occasions, however, the RAF pilots were un-lucky, as was the case with Squadron Leader Lockhart one night in November 1942. It had not been a successful mission for Lockhart because the weather had clamped down suddenly over France and he had been unable to find his landing ground. There was no alternative but to head for home with the agent still on board, and because of the weather conditions there was no question of making the trip at low level. Instead, the Lysander had to fly above a blanket of cloud, silhouetted like a moth in the brilliant moonlight.

It was not until he was over the French coast at St Malo, however, that Lockhart's troubles really began. Searchlight beams stabbed up through a break in the clouds and coned his Lysander, followed by heavy anti-aircraft fire. Lockhart and his passenger experienced an unpleasant couple of minutes as the Lysander twisted and turned. Then the flak died away astern and the aircraft set out over the channel.

Over Jersey, Lockhart began to relax. In a short time he would be landing at Tangmere and tucking into the traditional aircrew breakfast of bacon and eggs. He looked around, enjoying the calm tranquility of the moonlight – and at that moment an icy hand grasped his stomach. Arrowing down towards the Lysander's tail were two fast, powerful Focke-Wulf 190 fighters, with a third turning in steeply from the starboard quarters in case Lockhart tried to get away. Tracers flashed past the little aircraft's wings and in that split second Lockhart acted. In a simultaneous movement he closed the throttle and pulled back the stick. The Lysander shuddered, stalled and fell away in a spin towards the sheltering clouds below. The machine dropped into the opaque layer like a stone and Lockhart let her go on spinning for long seconds before applying stick and rudder to bring her out.

Emerging from the cloud base he was horrified to see that the Focke-Wulfs were still with him, closing in for the kill. It was now that the aircraft's manoeuvrability paid off. Opening the throttle, Lockhart sent it towards the sea in a screaming power dive, then pulled it up towards the clouds once more in a climb far steeper than anything the enemy fighters could follow. This time he stayed in the cloud until he was over the English coast, by which time the pursuing Focke-Wulfs had long since gone home.

One Lysander pilot who had more than his fair share of drama was Squadron Leader James Nesbitt-Dufort, who made history on the night of 4 September 1941 when he became the first pilot to land an agent in occupied France. He made the return trip with several yards of French telephone wire trailing from the Lysander's under-carriage. Several trips later, he set out on the night of 28 January 1942 to deliver another agent to a landing ground just south of the river Loire and pick up two more. The outward trip was accomplished without incident; the agents were exchanged and the Lysander was soon on its way home. Soon afterwards, however, Nesbitt-Dufort ran into trouble. Dense cloud forced him further and further down until he was flying at only seventy feet, hedge-hopping in blinding rain. Then ice began to form on the windscreen and the leading edges of the wings. Realizing that it was hopeless to fly on in those conditions, Nesbitt-

Dufort turned back into France, heading southwards until he reached the river Seine before turning once more on a course that would take him across the channel to Beachy Head. This time he tried to get above the cloud, climbing to 8000 feet through torrential rain. The icing, however, persisted, building up to a layer of three or four inches in depth on the leading edges of the wings. The Lysander's engine began to run roughly and although Nesbitt-Dufort gave it full power the aircraft refused to climb any higher. As the icing grew worse the aircraft became practically uncontrollable, wallowing through the sky and threatening to fall away in a spin at any moment.

A minute later the aircraft began to lose height rapidly. As there was little chance of making a successful forced landing, Nesbitt-Dufort decided to abandon the aircraft. However, he could not make the two French agents he was carrying understand that he wanted them to bail out, and with the altimeter unwinding at frightening speed there was no time to waste on explanations. As they were now over the coast again he decided that the only thing to do was turn back into France yet again and risk a landing.

Diving to pick up speed, Nesbitt-Dufort cautiously eased the Lysander round until it was flying on a reciprocal course. He continued to dive until the needle of the airspeed indicator reached 240 mph. Ice crackled from the wings and propeller with a noise like machine-gun fire, and as more of it dropped off the aircraft became easier to control. At 2,500 feet the pilot eased out of the dive, descending cautiously through cloud until he broke through the base at 1000 feet.

The Lysander was flying steadily now, but the huge cold front still barred its path to the north-west. It obscured the whole of the French coast from horizon to horizon, and Nesbitt-Dufort cruised backwards and forwards along it for more than a hundred miles, seeking in vain for a break. With no chance of getting through and the aircraft rapidly running out of fuel, Nesbitt-Dufort decided to fly back to the field where he had made the original pickup and see if he could deliver his two agents safely back to their resistance group. If he chanced a landing anywhere else, he reasoned, the odds were that they would all be captured.

He crossed the river Loire at Orleans and flew on south, heading for Chateauroux. He never made it. A few miles south of the river, the Lysander finally ran out of fuel.

Nesbitt-Dufort picked the likeliest looking field and brought the aircraft in for a landing. He had, however, failed to see the ditch that ran across the field. The Lysander's undercarriage went over the edge and there was a terrific crash as the machine came to rest on its nose, its tail sticking up in the air.

The three men staggered from the wreck with no worse injuries than a few cuts and bruises. All of them were exhausted by their ordeal in the storm, particularly Nesbitt-Dufort who had spent seven hours at the controls. An hour after leaving the wreck he stumbled into a hut beside a road and fell fast asleep. Nothing the agents could do would rouse him, so one of them decided to stay with him while the other went to get help from the nearest town. Luckily for all three the French resistance in this area was well organized and it was not long before a car arrived to take Nesbitt-Dufort and the other agent to a safe hiding place.

Nesbitt-Dufort remained in hiding for a month, the French family who sheltered him daily risking their lives to bring him food out of their own meagre rations. Then, on 1 March, came the news he had been waiting for. If weather conditions were right, he was told, an aircraft would take him back to England that night.

The second day of the war : Blenheim bombers, led by Flight Lieutenant Ken Doran, en route to their ill-fated mission to bomb the *Admiral Scheer*. Doran's skill and bravery on this occasion brought him the first Distinguished Flying Cross to be won in the Second World War.

Fairey Battle light bombers of the Advanced Air Striking Force who formed part of the frighteningly inadequate fleet of bombers which confronted the formidable strength of the Luftwaffe at Maastricht in 1940.

A Westland Lysander, specially modified with a long-range tank for secret flights to France.

Group Captain Percy Pickard and his navigator, Flight Lieutenant Alan Broadley, before the Amiens Prison raid.

Mosquitoes attacking the Gestapo Headquarters in Copenhagen.

James Stewart (seated), one of the few public figures who managed to get into combat, discussing plans for a mission with members of his crew.

ABOVE Liberator bombers flying over Ludwigshafen on their long and perilous return journey. James Stewart's quick thinking and courage on this mission saved an entire Bomb Group from total destruction.

LEFT 08.16 and thirty seconds, 6 August 1945: the only photograph ever taken from the ground of the Hiroshima explosion.

After a long and agonizing wait on a secret landing strip, Nesbitt-Dufort and the resistance men who had been looking after him heard the sound of aero engines approaching a few minutes after midnight. Recognition signals were flashed and the machine circled and came in to land. It was an Avro Anson, and as it taxied in the pilot poked his head out of the window and shouted a stream of friendly abuse at Nesbitt-Dufort in an Irish accent. It was none other than Squadron Leader Murphy, who had recovered from the wound in the neck he had received a few months earlier. With five agents and Nesbitt-Dufort on board Murphy succeeded in making a safe return trip to England.

No. 161 Squadron's activities increased greatly as the date for the Allied invasion of Europe approached in 1944 and continued long after the invasion had been successfully completed. In many ways the Allied landings brought additional dangers for the Special Duties pilots, for the invasion area lay along a stretch of coast over which many of their low-level routes passed.

In June 1944 the areas around the beachheads became so stiff with flak, both Allied and German, that it was virtually suicide to fly over them, as Lieutenant Haysing-Dahl – a Norwegian pilot with 161 Squadron – found to his cost on the night of 7 July 1944. Becoming lost in bad weather after a pickup, he inadvertently strayed into the beachhead area and was immediately greeted by an intense anti-aircraft barrage. The pilot was wounded in the hand and the aircraft was riddled with shell fragments.

The engine stopped, leaving no alternative but to ditch in the channel. With its fixed undercarriage the Lysander was a far from ideal aircraft in which to ditch, and on impact it immediately nosed under the water. The pilot managed to struggle out of the aircraft and then dived back beneath the surface to try and rescue the three agents who were still trapped in the machine. One of the men had drowned and another was so badly injured that he died within minutes. Haysing-Dahl and the third agent floated in the channel for two and a half hours before being picked up by an American torpedo boat.

With the invasion over and the Allied armies advancing through France, the main part of the Special Duties pilots task was at an end. Later, many of the pilots received high decorations from a grateful French government.

One of them was Wing Commander Bob Hodges, who had commanded No. 161 from 1943 to 1944. After the war he was summoned to the French Embassy in London to be invested with the Legion of Honour by Vincent Auriol, President of France. Auriol greeted him warmly, and as he pinned the decoration on Hodges' tunic the RAF officer wondered where he had seen the president's face before.

Then his mind went back to the night of 18 October 1943, and he remembered. On that night he had flown to a French airfield to pick up several senior resistance leaders who were on the run. One of them was the man who now stood before him.

DUEL IN
THE DARK

*It requires a particular kind of courage to fly alone over
enemy territory, deliberately inviting attack by night-
fighters. Yet that is what a small and gallant band of
RAF crews did, in order to ferret out the enemy's radar
secrets, and give the RAF's night-bombers a chance of
survival.*

ON THE NIGHT OF 30/31 JANUARY 1943, STIRLING and Halifax bombers of the RAF's Pathfinder Force led an attack on the German city of Hamburg. They bombed through cloud with the help of a new radar aid known as H2S. Five weeks later, Mosquitoes of No. 109 Squadron made the first use of another secret radio-navigation aid, code-named 'Oboe,' to make a precision attack on a power station in Holland.

The development of both these aids was just one aspect of a new form of air warfare that was becoming characteristic of the RAF's strategic bombing operations and the activities of the German night-fighters that opposed them: a secret war fought in the darkness, its weapons electronic pulses and radio waves. This war had really begun in earnest on the night of 27/28 February 1942, when Whitley bombers of the RAF dropped a force of British paratroops on a new and recently-detected German radar station at Bruneval. The paratroops were subsequently evacuated by the Royal Navy, taking with them key parts of the station's 'Würzburg' radar antenna, and examination of these by British experts led the way to the development of effective countermeasures.

In the summer of 1942, however, the nature and effectiveness of the Luftwaffe's airborne interception radar were still very much unknown quantities. In July, the

British radio monitoring service discovered that the enemy night-fighters over Holland were using a device code-named 'Emil Emil', but the exact nature of this device was not known.

A radio search detected signals apparently coming from the enemy equipment, but further information about it could only be gained in one way: by sending out special aircraft, fitted with radio detection equipment, over enemy territory. The crews of such aircraft faced an extremely hazardous mission, for to collect as much information as possible on the German device they had to allow themselves to be attacked by night-fighters fitted with it.

The task was assigned to one of the most secret units in the RAF, No. 1474 Flight. It was equipped with Vickers Wellington bombers, each of which carried highly-trained special signals operators whose radio detection equipment could pick up radar signals from enemy night-fighters that homed in on them. Once the enemy radar pulses were identified, the signals operators in the Wellingtons would radio the information they collected back to base – if they survived long enough.

In the autumn of 1942, the Wellingtons of 1474 Flight carried out seventeen lone missions over enemy territory without once being intercepted by a night-fighter. It was as though the Luftwaffe knew that the RAF was trying to secure its secrets, and was determined to give nothing away. For the British scientists, it was a frustrating time. A major RAF bombing offensive was planned for the winter of 1942–3, and unless some means could be found of jamming the new enemy airborne radar, it was certain that the German night-fighters would inflict heavy losses on Bomber Command.

Then came the night of 3 December, and No. 1474 Flight's eighteenth mission. The Wellington pilot on this occasion was Pilot Officer John Paulton. It was not his first mission over enemy-occupied Europe; he already had several operational trips to his credit, and each time he had managed to bring his aircraft safely home after avoiding the German flak and fighters. Tonight, however, was different. This was Paulton's first operational flight with No. 1474, and now, as he cruised around in the hostile darkness over Holland, seeking a rendezvous with an enemy night-fighter, he felt utterly alone and naked.

The mission seemed endless. For hours on end the Wellington flew in circles over enemy territory, roving in the vicinity of the German night-fighter airfields, a perfect target in the moonlit sky. Yet not a single fighter appeared. Apart from the occasional flash of a searchlight on the horizon, there was nothing to indicate that this was anything other than a peacetime training flight.

In the bomber's vibrating fuselage, Pilot Officer Jordan, the special signals officer, huddled over his radio detection equipment and listened intently for the tell-tale electronic sound that would indicate the approach of an enemy fighter. There was nothing except the crackle of static.

Paulton was just about to turn for home in disappointment when, shortly after four-thirty, Jordan gave a sudden yell over the intercom. He had picked up a faint signal on 487 Megacycles. It might be coming from a night-fighter's radar, but as yet he could not be sure.

A few moments later, however, there was no longer any doubt. The signals grew so intense that they drowned all other radio noise, which meant that a fighter was homing on to the Wellington – fast. Jordan warned the crew to prepare for an attack at any moment. The words were hardly out of his mouth when the Wellington's rear guns opened up with a clatter.

A split second later, cannon shells ripped into the bomber. Paulton shoved hard on the controls, sending the

Wellington into a violent diving turn. As he did so, the deadly black shape of a Junkers 88 night-fighter flashed over the cockpit with only feet to spare. The Junkers came boring in again, pouring more fire into the already hard-hit bomber. A cannon shell exploded in the fuselage, wounding Jordan in the jaw, arm and one eye. Despite his severe pain, he continued to draft a coded message to base, giving details of the signals he had picked up from the enemy fighter. Meanwhile, the Wellington plummeted from 14,000 to 500 feet in a crazy corkscrew dive as Paulton desperately tried to shake off his pursuer.

The Junkers attacked no fewer than eleven times, its shells and bullets ripping great holes in the Wellington's fabric covered wings and fuselage. Every one of the seven-man crew was wounded by flying splinters. Jordan went on operating his radio equipment, gathering more information about the fighter's radar, until he collapsed with the agony and loss of blood. The wireless operator, Sergeant Bigoray, was also badly hit in both legs by shell splinters. Nevertheless, he went on transmitting the coded message that Jordan had passed to him.

The bomber raced on at 500 feet over Holland, trailing long streamers of torn fabric. It was in a desperate plight; both throttles were jammed open, its gun turrets were out of action, and Paulton's instrument panel was shattered. Paulton, himself wounded, knew that if the fighter attacked just once more they would not stand a chance. There was no hope of taking further evasive action, no means of shooting back – and the bomber was too low for the crew to bail out.

Mercifully, the German pilot never delivered the final blow. The Junkers 88 vanished in the darkness and Paulton saw no more of it. Paulton's ordeal, however, was far from over. Although he knew that the battered Wellington might fall out of the sky at any moment, there could be no question of attempting a forced landing. The coded signals sent back to base by the wireless operator had not been acknowledged, and there was no way of knowing if they had in fact been received.

The one thought in Paulton's mind was that somehow he had to bring the aircraft back, so that the wounded Jordan could tell the full story to the 'boffins' back home. Fighting off his own pain and weakness, the injured pilot coaxed the crippled aircraft over the Channel. Miraculously, the Wellington stayed in the air – but only just.

Then, just as the coast of Kent came in sight, the overworked engines began to give up. With no chance of getting over the cliffs, Paulton ditched in the sea 200 yards off Deal. He and the rest of the crew were picked up safely by a rowing boat before the aircraft sank. All the gallant crew recovered from their wounds; for his part in the mission, Pilot Officer Jordan was awarded the Distinguished Service Order, while Paulton received the Distinguished Flying Cross and Sergeant Bigoray the Distinguished Flying Medal.

The gallantry of Paulton and his crew, and others like them, was to have incalculable consequences for the RAF's night-bombing effort. With the information the 'special' Wellingtons brought back, the British scientists were able to piece together an accurate picture of the enemy's latest night-fighter control techniques.

The German night defence system, known as the Kammhuber Line after the general in charge of nightfighters, in fact consisted of a massive searchlight belt some twenty-two miles deep. Ahead of it, stretching in a giant arc over the Low Countries, was a series of fighter control zones known as 'Himmelbett' zones, each one overlapping its neighbours. Within each Himmelbett zone was a radar station consisting of a 'Freya' early warning set and two 'Würzburg' sets, one for plotting the bomber and the other for directing the fighter on to it. After that, it was up to the fighter pilot, his observer and their airborne radar, code-named 'Lichtenstein'.

The British scientists now knew the frequencies of all the enemy radars, and set about devising a method of jamming them. The first countermeasure they devised was beautiful in its simplicity: strips of tinfoils, cut to the exact wavelength of the enemy radar and dropped in large bundles by the attacking bombers. Known as 'Window', it was dropped for the first time on the night of 23/24 July 1943, when 791 heavy bombers attacked Hamburg, and threw the German search radar into complete confusion. Each strip of tinfoil caused its own echo on the radar screen, effectively masking the movements of the RAF bombers.

The introduction of 'Window' drastically reduced RAF losses during the weeks that followed, dealing a crippling blow to the German system of close fighter control and bringing about a complete revision of night-fighter tactics. The enemy now adopted a new method of night interception known as *'Wilde Sau'* (Wild Boar), in which large numbers of fighters concentrated over the target cities and attacked the bombers visually without recourse to radar. To combat those night-fighters which still relied on radar interception, the RAF sent out long-range fighters – Beaufighters and Mosquitoes – to guard the flanks of the bomber stream.

These aircraft were fitted with a new homing device named 'Serrate', which, like Window, had been developed by the Telecommunications Research Establishment as a result of the information brought back by the special radio countermeasures aircraft; it enabled the British fighters to home on to the enemy's Lichtenstein airborne radar transmissions, and had a range of up to fifty miles. It was first used operationally in 1943 by No. 141

Squadron, which scored twenty-three kills in three months with its help.

Individual pilots who specialized in night-fighting, and whose aircraft were fitted with 'Serrate' and improved versions of airborne radar, took a fearful toll of the enemy. One of them was Flight Lieutenant George Esmond Jamieson, a young New Zealand pilot who, on the night of 29 July 1944, set up a night-fighting record that was never equalled. He was flying a Mosquito of No. 488 Squadron on patrol over Normandy, and his navigator was Flying Officer Norman Crookes. Jamieson's combat report tells part of the story:

I was patrolling the Coutance–St Lo area when I saw an unidentified aircraft approaching head-on at 5000 feet height. Against the dawn I saw that it was a Junkers 88 and as I turned hard to port I followed him as he skimmed through the cloud tops. I closed to 300 yards and there was a series of explosions from the ground caused by the Junkers dropping his bombs as he tried to get away. I gave two short bursts as we came to the next clear patch, and after a fire in the port engine and fuselage the Ju. 88 went down through the clouds vertically, hitting the ground near Caen.

As Jamieson looked down at the debris of the Ju. 88, Norman Crookes detected another aircraft on his radar and steered the pilot towards it. As he closed in, the unexpected happened: yet another Junkers suddenly burst out of the cloud, dead ahead of the Mosquito. The German pilot saw the danger and went into a diving turn, trying to regain the shelter of the clouds, but he was too late. Jamieson opened fire from a range of 350 yards, and flames were soon streaming back from the Junkers' starboard engine. The aircraft fell through the cloud layer, blazing like a torch, and plunged into the ground.

Within seconds, Jamieson and Crookes were on the track of another victim.

Almost immediately I obtained a brief visual on an aircraft crossing from port to starboard some 5000 feet away and identified it as a Ju. 88. My navigator confirmed this and took over on his ' box of tricks ', keeping me behind the enemy aircraft, which was now taking violent evasive action and at the same time jamming our equipment. When we were down to almost treetop height I regained the visual at only 250 yards, opening fire immediately and causing the Junkers to pull up almost vertically, turning to port with sparks and debris falling away. The Ju. eventually stalled and dived into a four-acre field where it exploded. This was near Lisieux and as the time was now 0515 hours I climbed back to 5000 feet and requested control to vector me back to any activity, as I had already observed further anti-aircraft fire through the clouds ahead.

The anti-aircraft fire, as it soon turned out, was barking at a Dornier 217, which spotted the Mosquito as it closed in and began a series of violent evasive manoeuvres. Just as the Dornier was about to plunge into cloud, Jamieson opened fire and saw his shells bursting on the enemy's fuselage. The Dornier went down, burning fiercely, its rear gunner – who must have been a very brave man – still shooting at the attacker. The bomber hit the ground and exploded.

Jamieson returned to New Zealand shortly after this exploit. His score was eleven enemy aircraft destroyed, one probably destroyed and two damaged, all of them at night or in weather conditions so bad that day fighters were unable to intercept. Eight of the enemy bombers had been shot down while trying to attack Allied forces in Normandy.

One of the pilots who roved over Germany in support of the RAF bombers was Flight Lieutenant James Benson of No. 157 Squadron. He also flew a Mosquito and his navigator was Squadron Leader Lewis Brandon. Together, they formed a highly successful team, as several

Luftwaffe night-fighter crews found to their cost.

On the night of 11 September 1944, Benson and Brandon were patrolling over the island of Seeland, off the south-east coast of Denmark, when Brandon picked up enemy airborne radar transmissions. A few moments later, he made contact with the hostile aircraft on his own radar, and steered Benson towards it. In the clear moonlight, the enemy was identified as a Junkers 188; it was flying in broad circles, apparently orbiting a German radio beacon.

Benson slid in astern of the 188 and hammered a long burst into it, seeing his 20-mm shells strike home on the night-fighter's starboard wing root. The 188 lost speed rapidly, its starboard engine bursting into flames, and Benson had to pull up sharply to avoid a collision. Looking down, the two airmen saw the 188 plunging earthwards, trailing a ribbon of fire.

At that moment, Brandon picked up another contact. It was a second Ju. 188, and it had probably been engaged in a night-fighting exercise with the first. Benson closed in rapidly and gave the Junkers a two-second burst; bright flames streamed back from the enemy's ruptured fuel tanks and it dropped away towards the Danish coast, shedding great chunks of flaming wreckage. The Mosquito sped through the cloud of smoke and debris that the Junkers left in its wake; when Benson and Brandon returned to base they found their aircraft smothered in oil and scarred by pieces of flying metal.

Most of the enemy night-fighters encountered by the roving Mosquito crews were Junkers 88s or 188s, Messerschmitt 110s or Dornier 217s. Occasionally, however, they encountered new types, specially designed for the night-fighting business.

It happened to Benson and Brandon on the night of 5 January 1945, over Northern Germany. They had been following a contact which, disappointingly, turned out to be a Lancaster when Brandon suddenly picked up another 'blip' on his radar screen. Whatever the strange aircraft was, it proved very hard to catch, climbing fast towards Hanover. Benson finally caught sight of it at a range of half a mile over the burning city; it was a Heinkel 219, a speedy, twin-engined fighter with a heavy armament, easily recognizable because of its twin fins and array of radar aerials.

Benson crept up on the enemy until he was 200 yards away and dead astern. The floor beneath his feet pounded with the recoil as he opened up with his four cannon, and the stink of cordite drifted into the cockpit. The shells slammed home in both the Heinkel's engines and large pieces flew back, causing Benson to break away hastily.

The Heinkel went down in a steep dive, one engine on fire, and the Mosquito followed it. At 6000 feet the enemy night-fighter entered a steep climb up to 12,000 feet, where it heeled over and dived almost vertically to the ground. The Mosquito crew saw it blow up. (Later, it was learned that the Heinkel 219 was equipped with ejection seats, the first aircraft in the world to use them. From the aircraft's erratic behaviour after its initial dive, it seemed that the crew of this particular 219 might have ejected successfully.)

Although the Germans made great efforts to bring new types of airborne radar into service during the last months of the war, the RAF managed to keep one step ahead throughout. Night after night, British radio counter-measures reduced the science of German fighter control to mere guesswork, causing a severe drop in morale among both controllers and night-fighter crews.

Had it not been for the continual radio jamming – and the activities of the Mosquito intruders – it is certain that the Luftwaffe would have inflicted appalling losses on

Bomber Command in 1944–5. That they failed to do so was a tribute to the gallant men who, two years earlier, had risked their lives to ferret out the enemy's radar secrets in the sky over darkened Europe.

TARGET: SUICIDE

Very early in the war, the RAF *found that daylight bombing missions without fighter escort were practically suicidal. When the Americans entered the war in Europe, however, they still had that lesson to learn – and their education proved a tragic and costly business.*

THEY CALLED THE TWIN-ENGINED MARTIN B-26
Maurader the 'Widowmaker', and it was true that when
it first entered service with the United States Army Air
Corps in 1941 it experienced more than its share of acci-
dents. The problem was that it was unusually heavy for a
twin-engined machine, and needed that little bit of extra
care in handling, particularly in the take-off and landing
configurations. It killed a lot of inexperienced pilots before
the Air Corps got used to it, and in its early days it earned
a totally unjustified reputation for being a lethal aircraft.

In action, however, with experienced crews, the B-26
was superb. It made its operational debut against the
Japanese in the spring of 1942, and soon excelled in the
low-level attack role.

The first Marauders arrived in the European theatre in
March 1943, equipping the 322nd Bombardment Group
of the Eighth Air Force's 3rd Bomb Wing at Great Saling,
near Braintree in Essex. The squadron immediately began
training for the same kind of operation the B-26 had
undertaken in the Pacific: low-level attack.

Many senior USAAF officers believed that it was a
serious mistake. The Japanese anti-aircraft defences in
New Guinea, they argued, were nothing in comparison
with the weight of metal the Germans could throw up
around objectives in Europe. The flak and the fighters
would tear the B-26s to pieces.

Despite these grim warnings, training continued unchecked and the first low-level mission was scheduled for 14 May 1943. The target was the Velsen power station at Ijmuiden, in Holland, which had twice been unsuccessfully attacked by the RAF. The American raid went ahead as planned; twelve B-26s set out, one aborted with engine trouble, and the remainder attacked the objective through intense flak at heights of between 100 and 300 feet. One B-26 was destroyed in a crash-landing on returning to base; the rest all got back safely, although every aircraft had suffered considerable battle damage. Nevertheless, the crews were jubilant; they had unloaded their delayed-action bombs squarely on the target, and they were convinced that it had been destroyed.

When reconnaissance photographs were developed the next day, however, the Americans were astonished. No damage at all had been inflicted on the power station. It appeared that the enemy had rushed special bomb disposal squads into the area to disarm the bombs, which had been fitted with thirty-minute fuses – standard practice in raids on industrial targets in occupied Europe, in order to give workers time to get clear.

The Headquarters of the 3rd Bomb Wing accordingly decided to mount a second operation against Ijmuiden on 17 May, although the commander of the 322nd – Lieutenant Colonel Robert M. Stillman – protested that another mission at low level against the same target was almost certain to end in disaster. HQ, however, was adamant; the mission had to be carried out, and Stillman had to do as he was told.

The Group's senior intelligence officer, Major Alfred H. von Kelnitz, also believed that a second attack on Ijmuiden would be suicidal. On the morning of the projected attack he wrote a strong memo entitled 'Extreme Danger in Contemplated Mission', in which he pointed out that after the RAF raids of 2 and 5 May, as well as the 322nd's attack on the fourteenth, the Germans would be ready and waiting. 'For God's sake,' he pleaded, 'get fighter cover!'

Fighter cover was not available, however, and Lieutenant Colonel Stillman, despite his misgivings, was forced to mount the attack without it. On the morning in question, 17 May, the Group could only put up eleven serviceable Marauders; six of these, led by Stillman himself, were to attack Ijmuiden, while the remaining five, led by Lieutenant Colonel W. R. Purinton, carried out a diversionary raid on another power station in Haarlem.

The first Marauder lifted away from Great Saling at ten fifty-six. The weather was perfect, with a cloudless sky and excellent visibility. The eleven aircraft formed up over the coast and headed out over the Channel at fifty feet, keeping low to get under the enemy radar coverage. Then, with the Dutch coast only thirty miles away, one of the Marauders in the second flight experienced complete electrical failure and was forced to turn back. As it winged over on a reciprocal course, it climbed to 1000 feet – just enough height for the German coastal radar on the Dutch islands to pick it up. The enemy now knew that a raid was coming in, and placed their fighter and anti-aircraft defences on full alert.

The remaining aircraft flew on, making landfall a few minutes later. As they approached the coast, great geysers of water suddenly erupted in their path as heavy coastal guns opened up. Lashed by spray, the Marauders sped through the bursts and spread out into elements of two in order to present a more difficult target, increasing speed as they did so.

As they crossed the coast, they were greeted by a storm of fire from weapons of every calibre, including rifles and light machine-guns. The Germans had 20-mm and 40-mm multi-barrel flak guns emplaced among the sand dunes, and from these glowing streams of shells arced up to meet the bombers. There was no chance of evasive action; everything happened too quickly for that.

In the leading aircraft, Stillman opened up with his nose guns, watching his bullets churning up fountains of sand and stones as they raced towards the enemy gun position ahead of him. There was a brief, vivid impression of grey-clad figures throwing up their arms and collapsing, then he was kicking the rudder bar and yawing the Maurauder to the left, his gunfire traversing the beach towards a second flak position.

The next instant, the world blew up in his face as a pattern of shells exploded all around the aircraft, knocking him momentarily senseless. The Marauder reared up, rolling uncontrollably, and Stillman came to just as it went over on its back. Out of the corner of his eye he saw his co-pilot, Lieutenant E. J. Resweber, slumped over the controls, either dead or badly wounded.

Frantically, Stillman worked the controls, fighting to bring the Marauder back on an even keel. It was no use. The stick flopped uselessly in his hands; a shell had severed the control cables. The B-26 righted itself briefly, then went into another savage roll. Stillman looked up to see sand and scrub whirling past, a few feet above the cockpit canopy. He put his hands over his face. It was his last conscious action.

German soldiers on the beach threw themselves flat as the Marauder hurtled over their heads, its engines still howling. On its back, it smashed into the sand dunes at over 200 mph, disintegrating in a great cloud of sand and smoke. Troops ran towards the debris, combing the wreckage for some sign of life. Miraculously, two men had survived the impact: Stillman and a gunner. Both men were badly knocked about, but they went on to recover in a German hospital.

Even as Stillman's aircraft was crashing, the flak was claiming more victims. Shells chewed into the starboard wing of Stillman's number two aircraft, and its pilot abruptly sheered off to the left to escape the line of fire. He broke right into the path of another B-26. There was a blinding flash, and suddenly the two machines were transformed into a ball of smoke and flame, shedding burning fragments as it rolled over and over towards the beaches. A third Marauder flew slap into the blazing cloud before its pilot had time to take avoiding action. Fragments slammed into it with the force of shrapnel; part of a wing dropped away and it spun down, out of control.

The wreckage of four out of six Marauders burned among the sand dunes. The two survivors of the first wave flew on bravely, intending to press home the attack, but a slight navigational error took them into the Amsterdam air defence zone and both were shot down by flak. Some crew members survived and were taken prisoner.

While the first wave was being massacred over the beaches, Lieutenant Colonel Purinton's flight of four Marauders managed to slip through with only relatively light damage. The formation, however, was scattered all over the sky, and by the time some measure of cohesion was re-established the aircraft had wandered several miles off course.

Vital minutes were lost while pilots and navigators searched for landmarks that would help them to establish a new track to the target. Nothing was recognizable in the flat, featureless Dutch landscape. At last, Purinton decided to abandon what was fast becoming a fruitless and fuel-consuming quest and asked his navigator, Lieutenant Jeffries, for a heading home.

As the Marauders swung round westwards, Jeffries gave

a sudden shout. He had seen what he believed to be the target, away to the south-west. A minute later, there was no longer any doubt: the navigator had spotted Haarlem.

The problem was that the Marauders had been briefed to hit the target from the south, where the anti-aircraft defences were lightest. Now they would have to make the attack from the north-east, running the gauntlet of heavy flak.

Undeterred, Purinton decided to press on. With flak of every calibre rising to enmesh them from all sides they swept towards the outskirts of the town. The power station was ahead of them, just where the target maps and photographs had told them it would be. One of the Marauders in the second pair veered away suddenly and dropped out of formation, trailing smoke. Its pilot dropped full flap, slid over a row of trees and stalled the bomber into a field. It bounced, shedding fragments, then slewed to a stop. The crew scrambled out with no worse injuries than a few bruises.

The other three Marauders roared over the power station and dropped their bombs. Their bellies glittered palely in the sun as they turned steeply to starboard, away from the murderous flak, and sped low down for the coast. Shellfire raked Purinton's aircraft, and with one engine chewed up by splinters and coughing smoke he knew he had no chance of making it home. He retained just enough control to slip over the coast and ditch the Marauder a few hundred yards offshore. He and his crew were picked up a few minutes later by a German launch. While they floated in their dinghy, they saw another B-26 hit the water and cartwheel violently. There were no survivors from that one.

Only one Marauder was left now. Its pilot, Captain Crane, pushed the throttles wide open and headed flat out for the open sea. He was too late. The Marauder's rear guns hammered as the deadly shapes of three Messerschmitt 109s came streaking down from above and behind. The fighters split up, one pair attacking from either flank and the third aircraft racing towards the bomber head-on. The Marauder was flying at only 150 feet but the Messerschmitt was lower still, its slipstream furrowing the sea. It opened fire and shells tore into the bomber's belly.

At the last moment the 109 climbed steeply, shooting past the Marauder and stall-turning to come down on the bomber's tail for the kill. The Marauder's tail gunner went on firing in short, accurate bursts, seeing his bullets strike home on the fighter's mottled fuselage. The 109 sheered off abruptly and headed for the shore, losing height.

Its last burst, however, had set fire to one of the Marauder's engines, and Crane could no longer maintain height. He made a valiant effort to ditch the aircraft in one piece, but it bounced heavily and broke up, the fuselage plunging under the surface like a torpedo. Only the engineer and rear gunner managed to get out. They found a dinghy bobbing among the islands of wreckage and pulled themselves aboard. It was to be their uncomfortable home for four days before they were finally picked up by a friendly vessel, the only survivors of the raid to come home.

Back at Great Saling, the 322nd's ground crews assembled at the dispersals and peered at the eastern sky for a sign of the returning aircraft. The first machine should have been back at twelve-fifty, but that time came and went and the tension grew as the minutes ticked away. Half an hour later, with the telephone lines buzzing as operations room staff rang other airfields to see if any Marauders had made emergency landings, everyone knew the grim truth. Not one of the bombers that had set out was coming back.

Of the fifty Americans who had set out on the mission, twenty-eight were dead. Twenty more, many of them wounded, were prisoners of the Germans, and two were safe. Stillman had been right; the raid had ended in disaster. But not even he had dreamed that it would be as bad as this.

There was one immediate result; no more low-level attack missions were flown by the Marauders in the European theatres. All subsequent operations were carried out at medium level, and the Marauder went on to become one of the most successful and hard-worked of all Allied medium bombers.

MOSQUITO MISSION

During the Second World War in Europe, fast, low-level attack missions by daylight became synonymous with one aircraft: the de Havilland Mosquito. This is the story of some of the more dramatic Mosquito missions, and the crews who carried them out.

30 JANUARY 1943 WAS A VERY SPECIAL DAY FOR Adolf Hitler. Exactly ten years earlier, he had brought the Nazi Party to power in Germany – and embarked on the path that was to lead to the holocaust of the Second World War.

The Nazis had planned big celebrations to mark their tenth anniversary. There was to be a huge military parade in Berlin, and Hitler himself would make a radio broadcast at eleven that morning. His propaganda minister, Josef Goebbels, would make another speech at four o'clock.

At eight-thirty, with the military parade already starting to assemble in Berlin, Hitler sat at breakfast and waded through the mound of telegrams and presents that had come flooding in from party members all over Germany. Unknown to the Führer, however, one present had yet to arrive.

It would be delivered in exactly two and a half hours' time – by the Royal Air Force.

The Germans had made no secret of their anniversary celebrations. Although Berlin had been raided many times at night, they believed that the RAF had no aircraft capable of striking at the capital by daylight and surviving.

They were wrong.

Five hundred miles from Berlin, three sleek aircraft were running up their engines on the RAF airfield of Marham, in Norfolk. They were twin-engined de Havilland Mosquitoes, the RAF's newest and fastest bombers. The Mosquitoes had entered service with No. 105 Squadron less than a year earlier, and had already carried out several daring low-level attacks on enemy targets. Now, on this January morning, No. 105 was going to take the war right into the heart of the Third Reich.

As the three Mosquitoes thundered away from Marham and set course eastwards, Squadron Leader Bob Reynolds – the man selected to lead the attack – was conscious that everything depended on split-second timing. The plan was to bomb the Berlin radio station, just off the Wilhelmstrasse, at exactly eleven o'clock, to coincide with the start of Hitler's speech. Reynold's navigator, Pilot Officer E. B. Sismore, was one of the best, and needed to be. Apart from the question of timing, the five-hour round trip would leave only a small margin of fuel. There was no room for error, or for a great deal of evasive action if they were attacked. The Mosquito bomber carried no defensive armament; it had to rely on its speed alone to evade enemy fighters.

The Mosquitoes raced across the North Sea at low level, climbing slightly as they crossed the German coast. The morning was brilliantly clear, and Sismore had no trouble in picking out landmarks as the bombers sped on. Reynolds climbed hard now, taking the three aircraft up to 20,000 feet for their final run towards the target. The lakes around Berlin came up under the nose, metallic patches glistening in the sunshine.

In Britain, linguists monitoring the German radio shortly before eleven o'clock heard an announcer tell the audience to stand by for an important speech. Then came the blow. The speech was to be made not by Hitler, but by

Hermann Goering, chief of the German Luftwaffe. Hitler, in fact, had developed a sore throat at the last minute, and Goering was standing in for him. The only consolation was that Goering was the next most important person in Germany after the Führer.

The Mosquitoes were over Berlin now. With thirty seconds to go, Sismore centred the broad ribbon of the Wilhelmstrasse in his bomb-sight. A few tufts of scattered flak burst around the speeding aircraft, but there was no sign of any fighters.

All over Germany, millions of people listened to their radios as a fanfare of trumpets died away and the announcer began to introduce Goering's speech. Suddenly, his words were cut short. Clearly, over the radio, came the heavy crump of exploding bombs as the 500-pounders dropped by the three Mosquitoes whistled down to erupt around the broadcasting station.

There was a long pause, punctuated by sounds of confused shouting in the background. Then, breathlessly, the announcer said that there would be some delay. His voice faded out and was replaced by martial music. It was nearly an hour before Goering finally came on the air. He was clearly harassed and angry. Only a couple of years earlier, he had announced confidently that no enemy aircraft would ever fly over the Third Reich. Now the RAF had visited the Reich's capital in broad daylight.

All three Mosquitoes returned safely to base – but for the RAF, the day's work was not yet over. Goebbels was due to speak at four o'clock, and a hot reception had been planned for him too. At twelve thirty-five three more Mosquitoes, this time drawn from No. 139 Squadron and led by Squadron Leader D. F. W. Darling, also took off from Marham. They flew at wave-top height to a point north of Heligoland, then turned in towards Lübeck. By this time the weather had deteriorated, and the aircraft ran through squalls along the whole of their route. The German defences too were on the alert, as the attackers soon discovered.

As the Mosquitoes climbed up to 20,000 feet Sergeant R. C. Fletcher, the navigator in the number two aircraft, shouted a warning: Messerschmitt 109s were attacking from astern. Fletcher's pilot, Sergeant J. Massey, and Flight Sergeant P. J. McGeehan, who was flying the third aircraft, both took violent evasive action and managed to shake off the fighters. Squadron Leader Darling was not so lucky. He was last seen diving down into cloud, apparently out of control, and failed to return from the mission.

The two remaining Mosquitoes flew on above a dense cloud layer. At five minutes to four they arrived over Berlin and Sergeant Massey dropped his bombs through a gap in the clouds. By this time the flak was intense, and it was another eight minutes before Flight Sergeant Mc-Geehan could get into position to make a successful bombing-run. His bombs burst half a mile south of the city centre.

As the Mosquitoes turned for home Goebbels' speech went out as planned – from the safety of an underground bunker.

Their noses down to gain speed, the two bombers raced for the coast, evading the worst of the flak and the swarm of Focke-Wulf 190s that tried to intercept them. They landed safely at Marham at six-thirty.

Although the Berlin raid had been audacious enough – and a foretaste of the day when the RAF and USAAF would be visiting the enemy capital constantly – it had been well within the Mosquito's capability in terms of performance. A longer mission had in fact been carried out only three days earlier, when nine Mosquitoes of Nos 105 and 139 Squadrons set out to raid the Burmeister and Wain submarine diesel engine works and shipyards at

Copenhagen, a round trip of 1,400 miles. The raid was led by Wing Commander Hughie Edwards, who in 1941 had made history by leading a squadron of Blenheims in a daring low-level daylight attack on Cologne – the first such mission against a target on German soil.

The outward trip across the North Sea was hard work, the Mosquitoes battling their way through cloud and heavy rain. Soon after crossing the enemy coast, where they were greeted by some very accurate flak, they suffered their first casualty when Flight Lieutenant J. Gordon experienced severe engine trouble and had to turn back. Pursued by streams of shells, he flew as fast as he could for the coast, hedge-hopping all the way. There was one particular nasty moment when the Mosquito gave a sudden violent lurch and almost dived into the ground; Gordon thought for an instant that he had been hit, but in fact his port wingtip had ripped through some telegraph wires. He made it back home and took part in the Berlin attack three days later.

Meanwhile, the remaining Mosquitoes bore down on Copenhagen. The rain had given way to bright sunshine and people thronged the streets of the Danish capital as the aircraft swept over their heads at a height of anything between 50 and 300 feet, often standing on their wingtips to avoid spires and tall chimneys.

The Mosquitoes raced over the harbour, heading for the island to the east of the city where their target was situated. Flak poured at them from shore batteries and ships in the harbour, the shells churning up water around the speeding aircraft. All the Mosquitoes came through unscathed and dropped their bombs in the target area, the crews observing a series of violent explosions. On the way out, a flak shell hit the aircraft flown by Sergeant Dawson and it dived into the ground. There were no survivors. Another flak-damaged Mosquito, flown by Sergeant Clare, struggled back to England only to crash on landing. The rest got down safely after a flight that had lasted five hours and thirteen minutes.

On 18 February 1944, the Mosquitoes carried out what was probably the most famous low-level daylight attack of all time when aircraft of No. 140 Wing, which was part of the recently-formed Second Tactical Air Force, bombed and destroyed the walls of Amiens Prison, allowing over 200 French resistance men to escape.

No. 140 Wing, which was commanded by Group Captain Percy Pickard, was very much a Commonwealth outfit, being made up of No. 21 Squadron RAF, No. 487 Squadron RNZAF and No. 464 Squadron RAAF. Six crews were selected from each squadron to make the attack, which was named 'Operation Renovate'.

The day fixed for the attack dawned overcast and grey, with storms of sleet sweeping across the Mosquitoes' base at Hunsdon. The forecast indicated that the route to the target would also be covered by heavy, low cloud. Nevertheless, it was decided that the attack was to go ahead, as many of the French prisoners were in danger of imminent execution.

The raid was to be led by No. 487 Squadron. At noon precisely, three Mosquitoes were to blast a hole in the eastern wall of the prison, while three more aircraft bombed the northern wall at three minutes past twelve. Then the Australians of 464 Squadron would go in, one section of three aircraft bombing the south-east corner of the prison while the other section attacked the north-east wing. The third squadron, No. 21, was to remain in reserve in case any of the other attacks failed. The RAF pilots were not happy about their watch-and-wait role, but all three squadrons had clamoured for first place in the raid and Pickard had settled on the easiest way to decide the order of attack – by the flip of a coin.

The three squadrons took off at eleven o'clock into the teeth of a blinding snowstorm, each aircraft carrying a pair of 500-pound bombs with eleven-second delayed action fuses. Over Littlehampton the Mosquitoes made rendezvous with their fighter escort, three squadrons of Typhoons, and headed out over the Channel at low level.

Despite the poor visibility Amiens proved easy to locate, the Mosquitoes skirting the town to the north and thundering towards their target along the straight, poplar-lined Albert–Amiens road. The New Zealand squadron attacked right on schedule, bombing from as low as fifty feet, and the leader's bombs slammed into the eastern wall about five feet off the ground. Meanwhile, the second section of three aircraft swept round to strike from the north.

Wing Commander R. W. Iredale, leading the first section of 464 Squadron, later gave this account of the attack:

From about four miles away I saw the prison and the first three aircraft nipping over the top. I knew then it was OK for me to go in. My squadron was to divide into two sections, one to open each end of the prison, and it was now that one half broke off and swept to attack the far end from the right. The rest of us carried on in tight formation. Four hundred yards before we got there, delayed action bombs went off and I saw they had breached the wall. Clouds of smoke and dust came up, but over the top I could still see the triangular gable of the prison – my aiming point for the end we were to open.

I released my bombs from ten feet and pulled up slap through the smoke over the prison roof. I looked round to the right and felt slightly relieved to see the other boys still two hundred yards short of the target and coming in dead on line. They bombed and we all got away OK, re-formed as a section, and made straight for base.

Pickard, meanwhile, who had gone in with the Australians, now broke off to act as master bomber. He flew low over the prison, examining the damage, and only when he was satisfied that all the objectives had been attained did he order the Mosquitoes of No. 21 Squadron to go home, their bombs still on board.

As the Mosquitoes roared away, prisoners – many of whom had escaped from their death cells with the help of explosives smuggled in by the resistance – streamed through the breaches in the walls and away across the snow-covered ground to the shelter of the woods beyond, where resistance workers were waiting for them. A massive German search operation later rounded up some of the fugitives, but many got clean away.

As the Mosquitoes sped away from the target, one of them – a No. 464 Squadron aircraft flown by Squadron Leader I. R. McRitchie – was hit by light flak near Albert and went down out of control. Pickard promptly turned back to fly over the wreck, presumably to see what had happened to the crew. His Mosquito was caught by a pair of Focke-Wulf 190s and shot down in flames. He and his navigator, Flight Lieutenant Alan Broadley, were killed instantly. All the other Mosquitoes returned safely to base.

Two months later, in what an Air Ministry bulletin described as ' probably the most brilliant feat of low-level precision bombing of the war ', the Mosquitoes struck again – this time against the Gestapo headquarters at The Hague, the nerve-centre of German operations against the resistance in the Low Countries. The HQ was a ninety-foot-high, five-storey building tightly wedged among other houses in the Schevengsche Weg, and it was strongly defended by light anti-aircraft weapons.

The task of destroying it was given to No. 613 Squadron, which was commanded by Wing Commander Bob Bateson. It would be the most difficult job a bomber squadron had ever had to face, and planning for the raid had to be meticulous. A scale model of the building was built, perfect in every detail right down to the thickness and composition of the walls, and scientists worked hard to develop a new bomb – a mixture of incendiary and high explosive – which was designed to have maximum effect on the masses of Gestapo files and records.

Bateson picked his crews carefully, and put them through weeks of intensive training. At last, everything was ready. In the early morning of 11 April 1944, Bateson led six Mosquitoes away from their base at Lasham, in Hampshire, and set course over the Channel.

As they approached the Dutch coast, Bateson and his navigator noticed something strange. There were no recognizable landmarks; they found themselves flying over a vast expanse of water, dotted with islands where no islands should have been. In fact, unknown to the aircrews, the Germans had opened the sluice gates on the River Scheldt, inundating a large area of the flat Dutch countryside. There was relief all round when, after flying on for a few more minutes, they finally got their bearings and learned that they were right on track for the objective.

As they approached The Hague the Mosquitoes split up into pairs, following in line astern, sweeping across the rooftops, the narrow streets shuddering to the din of their engines. Bateson's Mosquito streaked towards the target, bomb-doors open, its port wingtip missing the tall spire on top of the Peace Palace by inches.

Flight Lieutenant Peter Cobley, following Bateson, saw the leader's pair of bombs drop away. He had a hazy impression of a German sentry throwing away his rifle and running for his life, then he saw Bateson's bombs quite literally skip through the front door of the HQ. Cobley dropped his own bombs in turn, pulling up sharply over the roof of the building.

Two minutes later, with dense clouds of smoke already pouring from the shattered building, the second pair of Mosquitoes made their attack. After a further interval, the third pair finished the job.

The raid was a complete success. The Gestapo building had been completely destroyed, but the buildings that surrounded it had suffered only slight damage. All six Mosquitoes got back safely, without a shot being fired at them.

On 31 October 1944, another Gestapo Headquarters – at Aarhus, in Denmark – was attacked by twenty-five Mosquitoes of 140 Wing's Nos 21, 464 and 487 Squadrons, the units that had carried out the Amiens Prison raid. Led now by Wing Commander Bob Reynolds, they took off from Thorney Island and set out over the North Sea, escorted by eight Mustang fighters. The Mosquitoes carried a total of thirty-five 500-pound bombs fitted with eleven-second delayed action fuses.

The Gestapo HQ was located in two adjoining buildings which had previously formed part of the University of Aarhus, so once again there was the problem of making an effective attack while causing the minimum damage to other property.

The target area was reached without incident, the Mustang escort beating up trains and other targets of opportunity as they raced across Denmark at low level. The Mosquitoes swept across the Gestapo HQ like a whirlwind and unloaded their bombs into the centre of it, leaving it shattered and ablaze. One Mosquito actually hit the roof of the building, losing its tailwheel and half its port tailplane. It nevertheless managed to reach England safely, together with all the others. More than 200 Gestapo officials were killed in the attack, and all the files on the Dutch resistance movement were destroyed in the subsequent fire.

On 31 December Mosquitoes of No. 627 Squadron

carried out an equally successful attack on the Gestapo Headquarters in Oslo, and on 21 March 1945 it was once again the turn of the three squadrons of 140 Wing when Bob Bateson led them in a daring low-level attack on the main building of the Gestapo HQ in Copenhagen. Although the target was completely destroyed, the success of the mission was marred by the fact that one of the Mosquitoes, striking an obstacle with its wingtip, crashed on a convent school and killed eighty-seven children.

The Danes, however, were forgiving. Such tragedies, they said, inevitably happened in war. When Bob Bateson visited Denmark after the war, he was treated like a hero.

During his visit, he met several men who had actually been undergoing torture in the Copenhagen HQ when the Mosquitoes arrived overhead. They owed their lives to him. But that was all in the past; of far greater significance to Bateson was the day when he led his Mosquitoes over Copenhagen for the last time, taking part in a flypast to raise money for Danish orphan children, the victims of the tyranny he and his men had done so much to help stamp out.

BATTLE OF THE SECRET WEAPONS

In the summer of 1944, the war in the air took a new and frightening turn with the start of the German Flying Bomb offensive against Southern England.
To meet the menace, the RAF's first jet squadron was hastily formed and thrown into action. This is its story . . .

ON 6 JUNE 1944 ALLIED FORCES WENT ASHORE IN Normandy in the greatest amphibious operation in the history of warfare. Overhead, British and American fighter squadrons maintained constant patrols over the beach-heads, ensuring complete allied air supremacy. It had been a different story two years earlier, when Canadian forces had landed at Dieppe in 1942. On that disastrous occasion the Luftwaffe had been airborne in strength and whirling dogfights had spread out across the Channel; but now, as the allies consolidated their bridgehead, the allied air forces were complete masters of the sky.

One of the RAF units that helped to provide air cover over both Dieppe and the Normandy beach-heads was No. 616 (South Yorkshire) Squadron of the Auxiliary Air Force. Formed at Doncaster in November 1938 the Squadron had become operational in 1940 when, equipped with Spitfire MK. IIs, it had fought with distinction in the Battle of Britain and destroyed thirty enemy aircraft. In 1941 it re-equipped with Spitfire Vs, and under the leadership of Wing Commander Douglas Bader carried out several months of convoy patrols – a boring routine punctuated only by occasional fighter sweeps over the Continent.

In 1942 came Dieppe and a period of maximum effort for the Squadron. Afterwards it re-equipped with Spitfire

MK. VIIs which it used to intercept high-level reconnaissance aircraft operating over Britain at heights of up to 40,000 feet. Early in 1944 the main effort switched to escort duties, the Squadron's Spitfires accompanying British bombers which were attacking communications in France and the Low Countries as part of the bombing programme leading up to D-Day. During this period of operations the Spitfires also escorted allied medium bombers engaged in an intensive series of attacks on German V-I flying bomb sites along the Pas de Calais. The first V-Is, assigned to Flak Regiment 155W, had arrived at these sites in October 1943, but by the spring of 1944 the missiles had still not been produced in sufficient numbers to enable the projected massive flying bomb offensive against England – codenamed Operation Rumpelkammer – to begin, and the bombing attacks on the sites caused still further setbacks.

Nevertheless the first V-I was launched against London on the night of 12/13 June 1944, and although the carefully camouflaged V-I sites were kept under constant air attack it was apparent that the V-I offensive would not be curtailed until the sites were overrun by the allied ground forces, and with the latter still fighting hard to retain their foothold in Normandy it would be some weeks before this could be achieved.

As they patrolled the Normandy beach-heads in their Spitfires the pilots of 616 Squadron had no idea that they were destined to play a revolutionary part in the battle against the V-I flying bomb. Since the spring of 1944 there had been strong rumours that No. 616 was to re-equip with a radical new aircraft; most of the pilots however believed that if re-equipment did take place it would be with Spitfire MK. XIVs, and this belief was strengthened when, in June, two of these aircraft flew to 616's base at Culmhead. Then, suddenly, there was fresh

speculation when, in the middle of June, 616's commanding officer, Squadron Leader Andrew McDowall, and
five of the Squadron's pilots were sent on detachment to
Farnborough. It was not until they arrived that McDowall
and his colleagues learned what awaited them – a conversion course to Gloster Meteor F.1 jet fighters, the first
allocated to the RAF.

The prototype Meteor F.1 had flown in January 1944,
and twenty production aircraft had been ordered to meet
the urgent demand for an operational jet fighter for the
RAF. The F.1 was to be followed into service by the F.2
and F.3, of which twelve and sixty-six respectively were to
be completed by the end of the year. The two Meteors at
Farnborough, EE213 and EE214, proved delightful aircraft to fly and conversion progressed smoothly once the
pilots had got used to the idea of not having a propellor
in front of them. McDowall and the other five pilots on
the initial conversion course were enthusiastic about the
new aircraft and when they returned to Culmhead early
in July their eagerness quickly infected the rest of the
Squadron.

No. 616's first Meteor, EE219, arrived at Culmhead on
12 July 1944, the day on which, as a matter of coinci-
dence, the German V-I offensive began against Britain.
During the next few days, eleven more Meteors were
flown in from Farnborough and the task of converting
the rest of the Squadron's pilots to the new type continued. Without exception the pilots found the Meteor
delightful to handle. The main problem, after flying for
years in tailwheel aircraft, lay in getting used to the
tricycle undercarriage.

On 21 July the Squadron's Spitfires, accompanied by
two Meteors, flew to Manston where they were joined by
five more Meteors two days later. The pilots of the RAF's
first jet flight were the newly-promoted Wing Comman-

der McDowall, Wing Commander Wilson, Squadron Leader Watts, Flying Officer Roger, Flying Officer McKenzie, Flying Officer Clark, Flying Officer Dean and Warrant Officer Wilkes. The establishment of a Meteor flight at Manston was carried out in conditions of strict secrecy, a tight security cordon being thrown around the airfield. The pilots, now fully operational on the new type, waited impatiently for the chance to go into action.

On 27 July, No. 616 Squadron was ordered to carry out its first 'Diver' patrol, as the sorties against the V-I flying bombs were codenamed. The first pilot to take off at 14.30 was Flying Officer McKenzie, but he landed forty-five minutes later without having sighted any of the enemy missiles. Seven more sorties were flown during the course of the day with the same negative result. The week that followed was full of frustration and disappointment. In order to increase the time on patrol it was decided to decrease the distance between the squadron base and the approach path of the flying bombs by moving the Meteors to a dispersal aerodrome near Ashford, the aircraft carrying out their diver patrols from this location and returning to Manston at the end of the day's flying.

It was while flying from Ashford on 29 July that Squadron Leader Watts became the first of 616's pilots to sight a V-I. He spotted the missile after only ten minutes on patrol and closed in on it, but as he attacked his four 20mm cannon jammed after only two rounds had been fired. Helplessly, he could do nothing but sit in his cockpit and watch while the V-I flew relentlessly on towards its target. Later that day the same thing happened to another pilot, and it was subsequently established that the cause of the jamming was updraught in the cartridge case ejection slots under the fuselage.

The first real break came in the evening of 4 August when Flying Officer Dean sighted a V-I only minutes after taking off from Ashford. The enemy aircraft was some distance ahead and a few thousand feet lower down, and Dean eased the Meteor over into a gentle dive. As the speed built up to more than 450 knots and the distance between the two aircraft narrowed swiftly, Dean could see the unmistakable silhouette of the flying bomb clearly – the fat fuselage with its nose packed with a ton of high explosive, the short stubby wings and the long slim pulse jet engine with its sharp spurts of flame. Dean curved in behind the V-I until its orange jet exhaust was lined up squarely in his sights. The pilot throttled back. He knew that to approach too close to a V-I could be highly dangerous. He had read the combat reports of Spitfire and Tempest pilots who had been almost destroyed by the explosion of the V-I when their cannon shells had touched off the missile's warhead.

Dean pressed the firing button. A short burst of shells roared out from the Meteor's four cannon and then the guns jammed. The flying bomb streaked on, apparently undamaged. Dean pushed upon the throttles once more and brought his Meteor alongside the V-I. The pilot was determined not to let the flying bomb escape, but the two aircraft were racing over the countryside at nearly 450 knots and at that speed London was only five minutes flying time away. If Dean was going to act it had to be now, while the flying bomb was still over the open spaces of the downs. The question was, how? Suddenly, a daring plan came into Dean's mind. If it succeeded the V-I would dive harmlessly into the ground. If it failed, the flying bomb would crash anyway but he and his Meteor would probably crash with it. Juggling with the controls, he edged the Meteor closer to the speeding V-I. With infinite care he slid his wing tip under that of the missile, holding them just a few inches apart, then slowly he pushed the control column over to the left. The Meteor shuddered violently as the two wing tips stuck. Dean tensed, half expecting that the shock might cause the V-I to blow up. Instead, the flying bomb's wing lifted higher and higher until suddenly the V-I flicked sharply over on his back and dived earthwards. Dean watched it as it hurtled down, pulse jet still going flat out. Seconds later it exploded in open country in a gigantic mushroom of smoke.

Soaked in sweat, Dean set course for base. He had become the first British jet pilot to destroy an enemy aircraft and the Meteor, which was to remain the backbone of RAF Fighter Command for more than ten years had been blooded in combat. On landing at base Dean learned that another pilot, Flying Officer J. K. Roger, had also attacked and destroyed a flying bomb minutes after Dean's own victory. Roger's cannon had worked satisfactorily and the V-I had dived into the ground and exploded near Tenterton.

From now on the frequency of the diver patrols was stepped up considerably. No. 616 had two Meteors airborne continuously throughout the day, flying in relays in patrols of thirty minutes duration. By 10 August Dean had destroyed two more V-Is to complete his hat-trick and the Squadron's score mounted steadily. The busiest days were on 16 and 17 August when five V-Is were destroyed by the Meteor pilots. By 31 August 1944, the date when the V-I sites were finally overrun by allied ground forces, the Squadron's score stood at thirteen destroyed. Although it was only a fraction of the total number of the missiles destroyed by the British air defences, it nevertheless proved the Meteor's capability in action against small high-speed targets.

For the remainder of 1944, 616 Squadron settled down to a steady and somewhat boring routine of demonstration flights for the benefit of allied military dignitaries and air exercises in conjunction with RAF Bomber Command and the US 8th Air Force. The object of these exercises was primarily to assist the allied bomber commands to develop new defensive tactics against the German Messerschmitt 262 and 163 fighters which were appearing in action against the allied daylight bomber formations over Europe, and against which the piston-engined allied fighter escorts were virtually powerless. The new enemy aircraft could operate at very high altitude and had a speed advantage of as much as 100 mph in excess of the Spitfires, Mustangs and Thunderbolts which provided the bulk of the allied fighter escorts, and the allied air commanders quickly realized that unless a new set of tactics was devised the appearance of the enemy jets in substantial numbers would present a very real threat to allied air supremacy over Western Europe.

To give the United States 8th Air Force crews some experience of action against jet fighters a programme of air exercises was scheduled for the week between 10 and 17 October, with 616 Squadron co-operating with the USAAF 65th Fighter Wing and the 2nd Bombardment Division. For this task a detachment of four Meteors of 616 flew down to Debden under the leadership of the Commanding Officer, Wing Commander McDowall, who arrived at Debden two days earlier for a briefing session and to work out an exercise programme together with Brigadier General Jesse Orton, the Commanding General of the 2nd Bombardment Division. A detachment of four Meteors arrived at Debden on 9 October and the next day a formation of 120 B-24 Liberators and B-17 Flying Fortresses of the 2nd Air Division took off from their respective bases and made rendezvous with their fighter escort of P-47 Thunderbolts and P-51 Mustangs 9000 feet over Peterborough. In four tight boxes they set out over the exercise route, flying from Peterborough to Colchester, back to Peterborough, then heading north-west before finally turning on a reciprocal course towards East Anglia.

During the flight the four Meteors made a series of high-speed attacks on the formation, closing in on it from various angles at 450 knots indicated air speed and passing through the boxes of bombers before the fighter escorts had time to react. These hit and run tactics were extremely effective and were exactly the same as those employed by the German Messerschmitt 262 pilots. The only way to catch the fleeting jets was to step up the fighter escort at least 5000 feet above the bombers, which enabled the pilots of the Mustangs and Thunderbolts to build up speed by half rolling and diving in pursuit of the jet fighters. This method, however, involved very precise timing, and even if the Meteors were intercepted they were usually able to escape by virtue of their higher speed. Nevertheless, by the end of the week the American fighter pilots were achieving successful interceptions more and more frequently and valuable points on potential defensive measures were raised at the debriefing which followed every exercise. There were also lessons to be learned from the Meteor pilots' point of view, as these exercises presented the first real chance of pitting their aircraft in simulated combat against the most modern piston-engined fighter aircraft. Apart from a collapsed undercarriage and a burnt-out engine, serviceability of the jet fighters remained high during the exercise period and the ground crews gained valuable experience in turning round the aircraft in rapid time.

On 18 December 1944 616 Squadron received its first two Meteor F-3s, EE231 and EE232. Three more, EE233, 234 and 235 arrived on the twenty-fourth and in January 1945, following a move to Colerne in Wiltshire, the Squadron exchanged all its remaining F-1s for F-3s. On 20 January 1945, a flight of 616's Meteor F-3s flew to

Belgium to join number 84 Group of the 2nd Tactical Air Force at Nijmegen near Brussels. Because of the danger that anti-aircraft gunners and fighter pilots might confuse the Meteors with the Messerschmitt 262, the British fighters, which had been camouflaged in normal RAF day fighter colours, (lacking the black and white invasion stripes which were borne by most aircraft of the Tactical Air Force) were finished in a glossy white paint scheme overall.

The pilots of the Meteor flight, who had been looking forward to the move to the Continent and the action it promised were to be sadly disappointed, and the next few weeks were remarkable only for their lack of activity. Because of the risk of the Meteors falling into enemy hands the pilots were given strict instructions not to fly over enemy-occupied territory and instead they were assigned to fly standing patrols over Nijmegen and other allied air bases in the vicinity. To vary the boring routine the pilots set themselves unofficial competitions to see who could achieve the fastest scramble time, climb to altitude and so on. On one of these occasions during a competition to see who could get his wheels up the fastest during a formation take-off, Warrant Officer Wilkes retracted his undercarriage a split second too early with the result that the wheels came up before the Meteor was off the ground and the aircraft belly-landed. Operations from Nijmegen were carried out from semi-prepared grass strips or PSV matting, a fact that considerably alarmed representatives of Gloster Aircraft who visited the unit. Nevertheless the Meteor proved itself fully capable of operating under these conditions and on one occasion an aircraft was successfully flown out of a ploughed field after making an emergency landing.

The remainder of 616 Squadron arrived at Nijmegen on 31 March, and early in April the Air Ministry authorized the jet fighters to undertake a more offensive role. Although the Meteors made short forays into enemy territory, however, they failed to make contact with the Luftwaffe and it was decided to employ them on armed reconnaissance and ground attack. On 17 April, Flight Lieutenant Cooper became the first Meteor pilot to fire his guns in anger over enemy territory when in the course of an armed reconnaissance he sighted a large enemy truck near Ijiiden. After one firing pass the vehicle slewed off the road and burst into flames.

Meanwhile a second Meteor squadron had formed in the United Kingdom. This was No. 504 (County of Nottingham) Squadron Auxiliary Air Force, and after a short working-up period on the new aircraft it was declared operational and was sent to the Continent at the end of March 1945. As had been the case with 616, 504 Squadron was initially assigned to air defence duties before being released for ground attack in the middle of April.

For 616 Squadron the last weeks of the war in Europe were marked by feverish activity as the unit moved from airfield to airfield in the wake of the allied advance, carrying out its armed reconnaissance and attack sorties under considerable pressure. On April 24, four Meteors led by Wing Commander McDowall attacked an enemy airfield at Nordhalt near Cuxhaven, diving out of the sun from 8000 feet. In a single firing pass McDowall destroyed a Junkers 88 on the ground and sent some cannon shells through a motor vehicle. Flying Officer Wilson attacked two petrol bowsers which he set on fire and raked airfield installations with his remaining shells. Flying Officer Moon strafed a dozen railway trucks on the airfield perimeter and destroyed an anti-aircraft post while the fourth pilot, Flying Officer Clegg, shot up a large vehicle full of German troops who astonishingly waved and cheered as the jet fighter bore down on them, no doubt mistaking it for a Messerschmitt 262. They were still waving when Clegg opened fire at point blank range.

Up to now 616 Squadron had suffered no casualties while flying Meteors. It was a record that lasted until 29 April, when two Meteors flown by Squadron Leader Watts and Flight Sergeant Cartmell took off on an offensive patrol. Some minutes later the aircraft entered cloud in close formation and soon afterwards allied troops on the ground observed a large explosion followed by debris fluttering down. Neither pilot managed to bale out.

Although the Meteor pilots still half hoped that they would have a chance to test their aircraft in combat against the Luftwaffe's latest fighters, by the beginning of May it was apparent that this was not to be. Nevertheless ground attack work was exciting enough, for enemy flak was still heavy and several Meteors returned to base with battle damage. 4 May 1945 was destined to be the Squadron's last day of operations and came as a climax to a week of intensive ground attack activity. During the day's operations the pilots destroyed one enemy loco-motive and damaged another, knocking out ten trucks and two halftracks as well as strafing a number of in-stallations. At five o'clock, the Squadron received a signal to the effect that all offensive operations over Germany were to be suspended, and four days later came the un-conditional surrender of Germany.

Disappointed though they were at not having been able to engage the Luftwaffe in combat, the Meteor pilots' ground attack work had set the pattern for future Meteor operations in combat. Six years later the Meteor, flown by pilots of No. 77 Squadron, RAAF, was once again to prove its worth as a ground attack aircraft against a different enemy in Korea.

TARGET: PARIS

It was one of the most heart-rending missions any bomber crews had ever had to undertake. The target was Paris, and the crews were French.

THE PONT NATIONAL IS ONE OF THE BEST-KNOWN
of all the graceful bridges that curve across the River
Seine in the heart of Paris. Thousands of people – native
Parisians and tourists – cross it every day. A few pause,
midway over, to examine the twin plaques mounted on
the bridge wall. The inscription carved on them is brief,
easily read, and perhaps even more easily forgotten. '*A
la memoire des aviateurs français qui choisirent ici dans
les eaux du fleuve une mort certaine pour épargner Paris.*'
– In memory of the French airmen who chose certain
death here, in the waters of the river, in order to spare
Paris.

Their names are on the adjacent plaque, together with
the date of their passing: 3 October 1943. On that date,
every year, someone places a bouquet of flowers on the
wall above the plaque. The French remember their fallen,
and their heroes.

Behind those plaques on the Pont National lies a story
of courage and self-sacrifice. For it was on that October
day in 1943, for the first and only time in the Second
World War, that Frenchmen were ordered to bomb their
own capital city.

The crews of No. 342 (Lorraine) Squadron, Free French
Air Force, were a hard-bitten bunch – and they had a
score to settle with the enemy. Some of them had fought

in North Africa, supporting the British offensive in Cyrenaica in 1942, before being sent to England to reform early the following year. During the months that followed, the squadron, equipped with American-built Douglas Boston bombers, had specialized in attacks on precision targets such as power stations, marshalling yards, gun batteries and airfields in occupied Europe, earning a considerable reputation for itself.

Now, in the early morning of Sunday 3 October 1943, the crews anticipated just another routine daylight bombing mission as they filed into the briefing room on Hartford Bridge airfield (later renamed Blackbushe). As the intelligence officer pulled back the curtains that concealed the map at the far end of the room, however, a surprised murmur went up from the assembled airmen. A blackboard on the dais by the side of the map gave the target details: Latitude 48° 46' North, Longitude 02° 22' E. A red ribbon arrowed straight across the map from Hartford Bridge to the objective: Paris.

A blown-up photograph revealed the target in greater detail. It showed a section of Route Nationale No. 7, the main road leading from Paris to the French Riviera. Beside it, right in the middle of a built-up area on the outskirts of the capital, was the objective proper: the big power station at Chevilly Larue.

A hubbub of conversation broke out as the crews looked at one another, their eyebrows raised. It had been three weeks since they had last flown operationally, mainly because of bad weather, and they were restless and eager for another crack at the enemy. But they had not expected anything like this. It looked like being quite a show.

While the navigators went off to their separate briefing, No. 342's commander, Squadron Leader de Rancourt, explained the attack plan to the pilots, wireless operators and gunners. The raid was to be carried out by twelve

Bostons flying in three 'boxes' of four, the first led by de Rancourt himself. The outward flight was to be made at very low level – not more than 250 feet – and the first four aircraft were to drop their bombs from this height. The other eight Bostons were to stay low down until they were eight miles from the target, when they were to climb to 1,500 feet and drop their bombs on the explosions caused by the first four machines.

De Rancourt stressed that the attack on Chevilly had presented the Allies with a big headache. Not only was it heavily defended, but if French lives were lost in the raid the Germans would be presented with a major propaganda weapon. Only a week earlier, an American Liberator bomber had crashed into a Parisian department store, killing many innocent French people. The tragedy must not be repeated. That was why the RAF had given the job to 342 Squadron, many of whose crews had families in the Paris area. The idea was that the Frenchmen would go to extreme lengths to place their bombs squarely on the target.

The squadron intelligence officer, following de Rancourt, left the assembled crews in no doubt about the importance of the mission.

You are one of three squadrons which will today attack three power stations in France supplying the Paris–Orleans railway network, the Paris Ceinture, outer circle, railway, and also providing some of the electricity supply for Paris, the suburbs of Paris and Bordeaux. For the operation to succeed, the three power stations must be destroyed together. The Free French crews of 342 Squadron will have the honour of attacking the trickiest target: Chevilly Larue. No. 107 Squadron will bomb Chaigny power station near Orleans, and 88 Squadron a power station near Tours. The three squadrons will fly together as far as Essarts-le-Roi and will then separate and make their way singly to their respective targets. This is intended to put the enemy's observer corps off the scent. The whole operation will be carried out at very low level, without fighter cover, except on the way back, where you will be met by eight squadrons of Spitfires between Poix and Beauvais, two airfields occupied by German fighters. . . .

Weather conditions during the operation, the crews were told, would be good, with about three-tenths cumulus at 9000 feet and a visibility of fifteen miles in haze. One or two of the pilots exchanged wry glances; that meant the enemy fighters would have little trouble in locating them. Thank God for the Spitfires – if they turned up on time.

At twelve-fifty, as the Bostons taxied out for take-off, the crews remembered the message hammered home by Squadron Leader de Rancourt just before they boarded their aircraft.

Very close to the target are the working-class districts of Chemin Vert. It is essential that not even the smallest bomb splinter should hit them. At all costs avoid the houses; we must not endanger a single French life. If you are not absolutely sure, bring your bomb load back with you. If you are hit and you cannot get clear of the target area, you must do everything in your power to avoid crashing on the houses. You must try and crash-land on the Vincennes artillery ground – or dive into the Seine.

Apart from de Rancourt, who had the task of pinpointing the target for the remainder, no one was more conscious of the awful responsibility than Pierre Mendès-France, the navigator of the Boston that led the second two boxes. He was to drop the first bombs in the second wave, and if he missed the target by only a hundred yards, the bombs of the seven aircraft following him – dropping their loads on his signal – would pulverize the homes of French workers.

In tight formation the bombers streaked over the Channel, the waves blurring beneath them. At one twenty-five the French coast loomed out of the haze, and a few minutes later they swept inland over the rooftops of their landfall, Biville-sur-Mer. The bombers thundered over Normandy, flashing over the patchwork fields and the dark, wooded clumps of the bocage. In the hamlets that sped beneath their wings, people waved frantically as they caught sight of the roundels and the white Cross of Lorraine, symbol of de Gaulle's Fighting French, stamped on the Bostons' camouflage.

The Forest of Lyons was beneath them now, and beyond it the Seine. The formation roared on, leapfrogging pylons and high tension cables, and crossed the river at Mantes. The Bostons drummed up the Chevreuse valley, the din of their engines reverberating from the hillsides. So far, there had been no sign of either fighters or flak. They had been lucky.

Now, as the pilots and navigators peered ahead, familiar, much-loved landmarks began to emerge from the haze that hung over the horizon; the tall spire of the Eiffel Tower and the dome of the Sacre Coeur, the latter glinting whitely above the rooftops of Paris. Orly was dead ahead; the formation was right on track.

Over Saint Remy, with just over seven miles to run, the formation split up as planned, the leading four aircraft remaining at low level while the remainder climbed to 1,500 feet.

The low-level box of four Bostons howled down on Chevilly like a whirlwind, racing a few feet above the transformers and power lines with bomb-doors gaping open. The 500-pounders dropped away, and as the Bostons hurtled across the suburbs of the capital, de Rancourt mentally ticked off the seconds. On the count of eleven the delayed-action bombs exploded with a roar, sending columns of black smoke towering above the power station.

Further back, from his position in the nose of the Boston that led the second wave, Flight Lieutenant Mendès-France saw de Rancourt's bombs explode as the power station crept towards his own sights. The flak was coming up thick and fast now, but his pilot, Flying Officer Langer, held the Boston rock-steady. The aircraft shuddered to the recoil of machine-guns as the gunner opened up on some enemy battery he had sighted.

Seconds later, thirty-two 500-pound bombs whistled down as the Bostons dropped their loads into the smoke of the first explosions. Every bomb was right on target. The bombers turned for home, pursued by the flak. They ripped over Vincennes, where startled footballers hurled themselves flat as the Bostons tore across the pitch in a gale of slipstream.

Not all of them were lucky. One of the Bostons, piloted by Flying Officer Lucchesi, began to lag behind, trailing smoke. A flak shell had scored a hit on its starboard engine. Lucchesi, knowing that he could not make it home on one engine, put the crippled aircraft down on a patch of open ground in the Forest of Compiègne. It was a rough landing; the aircraft broke up on impact and all four crew members were injured. The navigator, d'Astier, had a badly broken leg and had to be dragged from the wreck seconds before it burst into flames. The gunner was trying to patch him up when a party of German soldiers arrived and took them both prisoner.

Lucchesi and his wireless operator, Flight Sergeant Marulli, were more fortunate. They had made their exit on the opposite side of the aircraft to the other two, and when they heard the Germans they lay low. Amazingly, once they had taken the navigator and gunner prisoner the Germans made no further search, so Lucchesi and Marulli were able to make their escape. A month later they reported back for duty with their squadron, having been smuggled out of France by the resistance.

One other Boston was missing. Flown by Flying Officer Lamy, its fate remained a mystery for twenty-four hours, until the British monitoring service picked up the following report broadcast by Paris Radio:

A week after an American bomber crashed into the Louvre department store, another plane hit by flak early yesterday afternoon came down in the very heart of Paris 100 yards from the Pont National. When the alert sounded, a group of Anglo-American planes was making for the southern suburbs of Paris. Their dirty work done, the pilots turned north towards Ivry. Above Ivry, one of the bombers went out of control, lost height but kept on its course. It skimmed a clump of trees a few hundred yards from the Pont National and then flew just above a pedestrian footpath. When it passed above the railway bridge, one of its wings struck a signal post. The plane was then violently knocked off course and 200 yards further on it exploded in the Seine, not far from Austerlitz Station.

This account was later corroborated by eye-witnesses. Flying Officer Lamy had remembered his co's words: dive into the Seine rather than endanger a single French life. Today, his name stands out on the plaque of Pont National, together with those of his fellow crew members: Warrant Officer Balcaen, Sergeant Rousserie and Sergeant Jouniaux.

The other ten Bostons flew on, low over the fields towards the French coast. Pilots and gunners scanned the sky anxiously, on the lookout for enemy fighters. In fact, the Germans had put up eighty Focke-Wulf 190s to intercept the Bostons on their way home, but instead they had encountered the eight Spitfire squadrons and a savage dogfight had developed over northern France. When it ended, the RAF had lost eight Spitfires and the Luftwaffe ten Focke-Wulfs, but the British fighters had served their purpose; the Bostons slipped out to sea unnoticed, the last aircraft touching down at Hartford Bridge shortly before three o'clock.

No. 342 Squadron's attack had been a devastating success. Coupled with a simultaneous attack on the station at Chaigny by 107 Squadron, it wiped out the Paris district's major source of power for several years. Right up until 1948, three years after the war, Paris had to rely on elderly, inefficient coal-burning power stations. In 1944, as the Allied armies advanced on the French capital, the German garrison there was deprived of power almost continuously, for the trains that were ferrying the necessary coal from the mines in northern France were being systematically destroyed by the Allied air forces.

As far as 342 Squadron's crews were concerned, the raid had been a success for a different reason. All their bombs had fallen well within the target area, and not a single French civilian life had been lost.

In 1954, the brand new power station at Chevilly was visited by the Prime Minister of France. During his tour, the Premier smiled as the power station's director enthused over his modern equipment. No one had told the director that his distinguished visitor, Pierre Mendès-France, had last taken a close look at Chevilly through a bomb-sight eleven years earlier.

THE LONG FLIGHT BACK

It was often difficult for men in the public eye to get into combat. One film star succeeded, however, and over Germany, in 1944, fought a battle that was more dramatic than a dozen action films rolled into one.

E*

THE FOCKE-WULFS CAME BORING IN, THEIR WINGS lit up by the wicked flashes of their cannon. A brilliant light filled the sky and a huge Liberator bomber staggered drunkenly, one wing wrapped in flames. A second later the wing folded up and tore away from the fuselage and the Liberator spun ponderously earthwards, leaving a great question mark of smoke staining the sky.

The pilot of a second Liberator, following immediately behind, gripped the control column tightly as his aircraft plunged through a cloud of smoke and drifting debris. For the hundredth time, he told himself that he must have been crazy to volunteer for combat flying, turning down a dozen cushy jobs in which he could have sat out the war comfortably, without danger. The generals had tried hard enough to get him to take those jobs; they had told him that he would be more use in publicity work than in flying a bomber over Germany. Getting on to operations had been a long, hard struggle for the pilot. His name was James Maitland Stewart.

Stewart, whose name was already a household word among cinema-goers, and whose performance in *The Philadelphia Story* had won him an Academy Award in 1940, had not waited for the Japanese attack on Pearl Harbour before volunteering for the US Army Air Corps. He had signed on as a private in March 1941, and imme-

diately had to fight a battle against the Hollywood cele-
brities and financiers who joined forces to obtain his
discharge, whether he liked it or not.

Stewart fought them all off, and began his flying training in the autumn of 1941. He already had over 100
hours' flying time as a private pilot behind him. But even
after he got his wings in January 1942, he still had to cope
with various Air Force generals who saw him only as an
ideal figure for the recruiting posters. For over a year he
was passed from one 'safe' posting to another, acting as
an instructor; all his requests for a transfer to a combat
unit were turned down.

While flying on one training mission in 1943, Stewart's
calm confidence saved both aircraft and crew from disaster. During a night flight in a four-engined B-24, there
was a sudden loud explosion as an engine blew up without
warning, setting the wing on fire. Chunks of debris
crashed through the fuselage, knocking out the trainee
pilot. Stewart had allowed the student navigator to sit in
the co-pilot's seat, and now the youngster sat frozen with
terror, unable to move.

Stewart acted quickly. Reaching out, he grabbed the
terrified navigator in his powerful hands and lifted him
bodily out of the seat. Then he gripped the controls in one
hand and punched the fire-extinguisher button until the
flames went out, afterwards bringing the aircraft back to
base for a three-engined landing.

Soon after this incident, to his amazement and delight,
Stewart got his wish and was posted as operations officer
to the 703rd Squadron of the 445th Bomb Group. In
November 1943 the film star found himself winging his
way over the Atlantic with the rest of the group, bound
for Tibenham in Norfolk, where the 445th was to become
part of the US 8th Air Force in Britain.

During December, the group made two raids on Germany – the first on the thirteenth, when the Liberators attacked the u-boat pens at Kiel. Stewart flew on both missions and got his first taste of action, but bad weather put a stop to further operations for two weeks.

Then came 7 January 1944, the day when Captain James Stewart became a real-life hero. At ten o'clock that morning, five hundred Liberators and Flying Fortresses assembled over East Anglia and set course out over the North Sea. There were ten Bomb Groups in all, and Stewart was leading the 445th.

The first German fighters hit them over Belgium, an avalanche of Messerschmitts and Focke-Wulfs tumbling out of the sun and ripping through the massed American formation. Smoke-trails criss-crossed the sky as burning aircraft spun down. The remainder closed up the gaps in their ranks and droned on, heading for Frankfurt. More fighters came in, and more aircraft were lost, but so far the 445th Bomb Group had come through unharmed. Suddenly, the whole huge bomber formation altered course, wheeling across the sky towards the real target – Ludwigshafen. The course the leading bombers had been following towards Frankfurt had been a feint, designed to confuse the German fighter controllers. The bomber groups now split up, each one making its own way to the target. Stewart's group began the run-in, the bombers lurching through heavy anti-aircraft fire. The bomb-doors of Stewart's Liberator swung open – and at that moment a shell exploded under the port wing, sending the aircraft in a violent roll to starboard. Sweating, Stewart fought with the controls, bringing the damaged bomber back to level flight once more. A minute later, the forty-eight Liberators of his group released their bombs and turned for home, chased by the flak.

But the 445th Bomb Group's ordeal was just beginning. As Ludwigshafen fell behind, Stewart noticed another group of bombers away to the west – badly off course and apparently heading for home by a route that would take them over northern France, which was stiff with fighters and flak. A lesser man might have left them to their fate in his haste to get away from those deadly skies, but James Stewart was not that kind. Without hesitation, he ordered the pilots of his group to increase speed and catch up with the straying bombers; the extra fire-power of his forty-eight Liberators could spell the difference between survival and disaster.

As he got closer, Stewart identified the other Liberator group as the 389th; its leader, a major, was a friend of his. Stewart tried to call him up over the R/T, but failed to make contact. Ordering his own group to close up into tight formation, he swung the bombers in until they were flying directly behind the 389th and slightly below. In this way, if any fighters tried to pick off the other group's 'tail-end charlies', they would run into the fire of dozens of machine-guns from the 445th's aircraft.

Time ticked by with agonizing slowness. The afternoon sun blazed down out of a clear sky; the only cloud was a few wisps of cirrus, thousands of feet higher up. So far, miraculously, the German fighters had made no attempt to interfere: apart from the Liberators and scattered tufts of flak, the sky was empty.

It was too good to last. Thirty miles south-west of Paris, there was a sudden flash of sunlight on a wing high above. Straining his eyes, Stewart made out a shoal of glittering crosses arcing across the sky towards the bomber formation; Messerschmitts and Focke-Wulfs, thirty or forty of them. The enemy fighters split up into flights of three, attacking from several different directions. Cordite fumes drifted through Stewart's Liberator as his gunners opened up, pumping their heavy point-five bullets at the fighters that flashed overhead. A Messerschmitt, caught in a cone of fire from the guns of four aircraft, flew apart like matchwood; the bits fluttered down, turning over and over.

It was then that the leading Liberator of the 389th was hit and blew up, spiralling earthwards in a mushroom of smoke through which the 445th's bombers flew seconds later. Stewart watched helplessly as the blazing aluminium coffin dwindled against the French countryside; there were no parachutes.

More fighters came in; there was a flurry of tracer and a second Liberator in the leading group turned over on its back and went down vertically towards the ground. A minute later it was followed by another, its tail unit torn off by a hail of 20-mm shells. There was a short lull, and then the fighters came in again, the Luftwaffe pilots hurling themselves through the curtain of fire from the bombers' guns with no apparent thought for their own safety. Several were shot down, but two more of the 389th's Liberators crashed in flames.

Some aircraft in the leading group began to straggle; over the radio, Stewart warned his own pilots once again to keep close together so that the guns of each aircraft could cover its neighbours. It was their only chance. But even as his pilots obeyed and jockeyed for position another of the 389th's Liberators went down – and then another. . . .

The American pilots could see the French coast now – the most welcome sight they had even seen. As they approached it, the German fighters made one more all-out attack before breaking off, short of fuel and ammunition – but not before an eighth Liberator's wreckage had been scattered over the snow-covered French fields below.

Suddenly, Stewart caught sight of more black dots racing towards them from the north. The gunners tensed behind their weapons, fingers on the triggers – and then relaxed, laughing and joking in their relief, as they recognized the graceful shapes of Spitfires.

Two hours later, Stewart led the 445th Bomb Group in to land at Tibenham; not a single aircraft had been lost. Later, an official citation was to credit him with saving the battered 389th Bomb Group from complete destruction, thanks to his decision to escort it clear of enemy territory.

James Stewart ended the war with the rank of lieutenant-colonel, having flown twenty missions over Germany and won a Distinguished Flying Cross. Since then, Stewart has fought in many different 'wars' – in front of the Hollywood film cameras. So have many of his colleagues, but unlike most of them, James Stewart had the experience of fighting in a real-life shooting war, in the embattled skies of Europe.

LAST FLIGHT FROM BERLIN

It needed courage to fly into besieged Berlin, under fire by Russian guns from all sides. But it needed even more courage to force SS officers out of an aircraft at gunpoint, in order to evacuate wounded soldiers.

MAJOR WOLFGANG KLEMUSCH'S HAND TREMBLED slightly as he studied the secret typewritten orders which had just been handed to him. Instinctively he knew that this was going to be a dangerous mission, perhaps the most dangerous he had ever been called upon to undertake.

Klemusch, a pilot with the Luftwaffe's 131st Long-Range Maritime Reconnaissance Squadron, based at Copenhagen, was no stranger to peril. For most of the war the squadron's task, equipped with lumbering three-engined Blohm and Voss BV.138 flying boats, had been to shadow the allied convoys which were taking vital war supplies round the north coast of Norway to the Russian port of Murmansk, a theatre of operations where the weather had proved to be a worse enemy than enemy action. Many of Klemusch's friends had failed to return from these missions, their bodies lost for ever in the freezing waters beyond the Arctic Circle.

Such was the price that had to be paid in war, but this time it was different. This was 1 May 1945, and Hitler's Germany was collapsing in ruins. Berlin, the German capital, was already surrounded by Soviet forces, while from the west the Anglo-American armies were spearing deep into the heart of north, central and southern Germany. The end could only be a matter of days away.

Nothing seemed worth dying for now, but orders were orders and they had to be carried out.

The orders that Klemusch read over and over again were simple enough.

You are to fly to Berlin. There you will make rendezvous with a special courier group from the Führer Headquarters, who will identify themselves to you by the code word *Johannmeier*. Rendezvous is to be made on the eastern bank of the Wannsee at 0100 hours, where the group's location will be signalled by flashing searchlights. You are to take the couriers on board and fly them to Lake Schwerin, where you will make rendezvous on the west bank with a motorized column. You will disembark the couriers and ensure their safe delivery to this column. You are then to return to base. Moonlight conditions may be expected for your landing on the Wannsee and Lake Schwerin. The mission must be completed by daybreak.

It was simple enough in essence, but it meant a pin-point landing behind the Russian lines with very little in the way of navigation aids. There were not even any charts; Klemusch had to make do with a map of northern Germany torn out of a school atlas. Klemusch called his crew together for a briefing at eleven-thirty that night. Although he himself was not the pilot on this occasion, he was nevertheless still the aircraft commander, a not un-usual procedure in the wartime Luftwaffe.

At exactly eleven fifty-eight the BV.138 churned its way across the sea and lifted into the darkened sky, heading down the Danish coast. It crossed the north German coast near Warnemünde at less than a thousand feet, keeping low to avoid detection by any marauding Russian night-fighters. Away in the distance the crew could see the town of Wittenberge. Here, the Americans were forging their bridgehead across the River Elbe, and the sky in that direction was lit up by flashes of artillery fire.

As they approached Berlin the crew gazed in horror at

the scene that unfolded beneath them. The whole earth seemed to be in flames. The sky above the outskirts of the city itself was thick with sparks and ashes. The cockpit filled with smoke permeated with the sickly stench of roasting flesh. Berlin, which had once been one of the most beautiful cities in Europe, was now a huge furnace, the rivers of fire than ran through its shattered streets punctuated by the sudden vivid flashes of shellbursts as Russian guns pounded the last pockets of German resistance.

The flying boat droned on past the shattered city, turning in from the south. Over the southern outskirts the sky suddenly erupted in a whirlwind of anti-aircraft fire and probing searchlights stabbed upwards, threatening to ensnare the machine in a web of light. Sweating with fear and half blinded by the searchlights and the glare of burning buildings, the pilot took the BV.138 down in a screaming dive almost to ground level, racing along the line of the river Havel in a northerly direction.

Klemusch strained his eyes ahead, striving to pick out landmarks, but in this holocaust of flame and smoke it was difficult to distinguish anything. All he could do was follow the river and hope for the best. Then, suddenly, a curious and almost terrifying sight materialized ahead and slightly off to starboard. It looked for all the world like a glistening patch of blood, emerging from the lurid darkness. Klemusch breathed a sigh of relief as he recognized it for what it was. It was one of the lakes on the river Havel, its flat surface reflecting the fires of Berlin. A minute later he was able to make out their destination, the Wannsee, the lake which before the war had been a favourite rendezvous for German high society. He tapped the pilot's shoulder and the pilot acknowledged that he too had seen the lake. He brought the BV.138 in for a straight approach, flattening out over the lurid water. The flying boat's hull made contact but the speed was too high and the big machine bounced back into the air again, hanging helplessly for long seconds before splashing down for good and churning across the lake in a great wake of foam.

At that moment searchlights flashed out from the darkened shore of the lake and Klemusch ordered the pilot to taxi towards them, recalling his orders. Then, without warning, parachute flares arced up into the sky and burst over the lake, flooding the whole scene with their stark, pitiless light. Seconds later the BV.138 came under fire from almost every side. Machine-gun bullets chattered around the big boat and shells erupted alongside, raising fountains of water. In the light of the flares Klemusch could now see dark humped shapes on the shore of the lake and recognized them as tanks. So the Russians had advanced this far already.

The flying boat shuddered as bullets and splinters smashed through it. Both radio operator and flight engineer reported that they had been slightly wounded. Klemusch ordered his crew to fire back with everything they had. He himself dived into a gun turret and raked the shore with bursts from one of the 138's 20-millimetre cannon. The pilot meanwhile turned away from the danger and taxied for the shadowy further shore of the lake, pursued by more streams of machine-gun fire. Then, miraculously, the Russian gunfire died away and the flying boat drifted in an eerie silence.

Klemusch took advantage of the unexpected lull to take stock of the situation. The picture that presented itself was far from encouraging. For a start there was no sign of the promised moonlight, which meant that it was difficult to make out any detail at all on the banks of the lake. But one thing was certain; the flying boat had been ordered to make rendezvous with the couriers on the east bank of the Wannsee, and that was exactly where most of the enemy fire was coming from. It was obvious that the plan would have to be changed – assuming of course that a plan still existed at all.

Suddenly there was a fresh alarm as one of the crew members spotted the dark shapes of small boats creeping over the water towards the flying boat. Klemusch ordered his gunners to be ready; the boats might be manned by Germans who had taken to the water to try and escape the enemy, or they could be full of Russians armed with machine-guns and hand grenades, bent on the flying boat's destruction. Klemusch leaned out of the starboard hatch and drew his pistol, pointing it at the occupants of the nearest boat. They seemed to be civilians and they called out to him in German, but that meant nothing. At this stage of the game he dare not take any risks. His gunners stayed on the alert as the boat came closer.

Three of the boat's occupants indicated that they wished to come aboard. Klemusch helped them through the hatch, keeping them covered all the time.

Inside the flying boat the leader of the three snapped to attention and announced that they were ss staff officers who had taken refuge on one of the islands in the lake. The Russians, he said, were everywhere. As soon as it was dawn they would wipe out everything on the lake and around it. A note of cold authority came into the speaker's voice. Klemusch, he said, was to take off without further delay and fly north with the ss officers on board.

Klemusch looked at the man. He did not like the ss and he liked officers who ran away from their posts dressed in civilian clothes even less. 'I am sorry,' he said, 'but you have produced no identification, and anyway I have a mission to carry out. You may return to your posts, put on your uniforms and then come back. Until then, however, my answer is no.'

The ss men held a whispered conference among themselves. When their leader turned back to Klemusch his attitude was full of menace. It was a dangerous situation and Klemusch lost no time in asserting his authority. Ramming the muzzle of his pistol in the ss man's stomach, he ordered him and his colleagues back into their boat. Muttering threats and curses they had no choice but to obey. One of Klemusch's crewmen kept a machine-gun trained on the craft until it vanished in the night.

Klemusch decided to taxi towards the east bank again to see if he could pick up any sign of the couriers. As the flying boat forged slowly ahead, however, it ran into another storm of machine-gun fire and the pilot sheered hastily away. Since none of the crew members had seen anything that looked like a recognizable signal, Klemusch decided that the couriers must have been prevented from reaching the rendezvous by the Soviet forces. It now appeared impossible to carry out his primary mission, so instead he made up his mind to try and evacuate as many refugees as possible from inside the Russian trap.

More boats converged on the flying boat out of the darkness and Klemusch ordered the flight engineer to shut down all engines in case one of the small craft ran into a propellor with disastrous consequences. The boats were full of wounded soldiers, mostly from the Wannsee Marine Brigade, who had been hauled out of a military hospital in Berlin to strengthen the faltering German defences. Their cries for help were pitiful and the Luftwaffe crew watched helplessly as several boats overturned, sending their struggling occupants into the water. Klemusch lost no time in taking on some of the worst cases, although with five crew members already on board the BV.138 and a restricted take-off distance, he was strictly limited in the number he dare carry. Ten soldiers was the absolute limit, and when that number had been reached the crew had to shut their ears to the cries of those who still drifted on the lake.

Klemusch ordered the flight engineer to restart the engines, and now another crisis presented itself. When the starter switches were engaged nothing happened. It appeared that the firing of the flying boat's electrically operated machine-guns had drained all power from the batteries. Klemusch's heart sank. The BV.138 was as helpless as a crippled bird. With the coming of dawn, Russian guns would blast her out of the water.

He decided to abandon the flying boat, leaving delayed action demolition charges on board, and make his way westwards with his crew, putting as much distance as possible between themselves and the Russians before daybreak. Then, as the crew supervised the preparation of the demolition charges, Klemusch had a sudden brainwave. He remembered that the BV.138 carried a small auxiliary generator designed to give emergency power to the accumulators. He had forgotten all about it for the simple reason that he had never used it. Most BV.138 crews who had used the device maintained that it had never worked satisfactorily. Now, Klemusch thought wryly, was the time to find out whether their claim were true or not.

It would not be easy. It was a good two hours since the engines had been shut down and they were cold, which meant that just that much extra current would be needed to turn them over.

Nevertheless, Klemusch knew that it was their only chance. He ordered the crew to close down all non-essential electrical equipment. The voltameter still read zero, but he breathed a silent prayer and pulled the starter knob for the starboard engine.

Again nothing happened. Apart from the hum of the emergency generator, everything was silent. Suddenly, without warning, the starboard propeller gave a single turn. Frantically, Klemusch pumped the throttle lever. The engine gave a couple of bangs then burst into full-throated life. With electric current now flowing once more it was soon possible to restart the other two engines.

Klemusch knew that it would need several hours flying at high rpm before the batteries received anything like a normal charge. There could be no question of shutting down the motor again or of remaining on the Wannsee any longer. It was now after four o'clock and the first streaks of dawn were beginning to appear through the veil of smoke and dust that hung across the eastern sky. Already, sporadic enemy machine-gun fire was chattering out from the far shore, probing for the still invisible flying boat.

With the danger growing every minute, Klemusch ordered his pilot to take off. The flying boat lifted away from the lake, keeping low to avoid the bursts of fire that still pursued it. The pilot set course north-westwards for the river Elbe, then turned northwards towards the Baltic coast. It was growing daylight now, and the crew kept their eyes peeled for signs of Allied fighters. The river Elbe marked the junction between the foremost Russian and American forces and there was normally intense air activity in this area. If the fighters caught them they would stand no chance of survival.

The menace from enemy fighters, however, was not the only problem the Germans had to face. As the BV.138 flew on the oil pressure warning light suddenly glowed on the instrument panel. A minute later the flight engineer told Klemusch that both the oil and coolant pipes had been shot through by machine-gun fire and that one of the aircraft's twin tail-booms was riddled like a sieve. The aircraft in fact was in such a condition that it was doubtful whether it would be able to reach Copenhagen. There was nothing for it but to hang on and hope for the best, keeping as low as possible and flying from lake to lake across northern Germany. If the aircraft began to break up the pilot could only do his best and try to put it down as quickly as possible in one piece.

Now, for the first time, Klemusch had a chance to talk to the soldiers he had taken on board. All were wounded, some seriously. One or two seized his hand in gratitude, tears streaming unashamedly down their faces. A couple of hours earlier their only prospect had been capture by the Russians and, more than likely, years in a prison camp. Now, miraculously, they were on their way to safety. Their faces told Klemusch that he had been right in his decision to abandon a hopeless mission in favour of a little humanity.

Amazingly, the bullet-riddled BV.138 held together. Ninety minutes later the pilot made a safe landing in the sea off Copenhagen. Klemusch kept silent about his treatment of the ss officers. He knew that if the news leaked out he would face a firing squad. In the event he need not have worried. The war in Europe ended a week later and then it was the ss who were the fugitives.

It was not until a long time later that Klemusch learned that he had made the last flight of any German aircraft from the besieged city of Berlin. He learned, too, the real reason for his mission. The couriers he was to have picked up carried with them the last Will and Testament of Adolf Hitler, who had committed suicide in his Berlin bunker the day before, 30 April. Unknown to Klemusch, the men he had forced from his flying boat at gunpoint were, in fact, the couriers. They were Major Willi Johannmeier, ss *Standartenführer* Wilhelm Zander and Hitler's last press adjutant, Heinz Lorenz. Their task was to take the will to Flensburg where it was to have been instrumental in forming a new Nazi leadership. As it was, the will was lost for several months. When it finally came to light it was used as evidence in the Nuremberg War Crimes Trials in 1946.

Klemusch's flight from Berlin had made history, though not in the way the Nazi leadership had anticipated. Instead of unwittingly helping to spread the gospel of the Nazi creed, he had given ten wounded soldiers a chance of life. Looking back, it seemed a very fair exchange.

THE
LAST vc

*The atomic bombs had fallen on Japan, and the end of
the war was only days away. It seemed senseless to risk
one's life in a lone attack on heavily defended Japanese
warships. But that was Lieutenant Robert Gray's duty,
and he carried it out without hesitation.*

THE FOUR CORSAIR FIGHTERS OF NO. 1841 Squadron, Fleet Air Arm, skimmed over the shimmering, glassy waters of the Pacific. Far behind them, the aircraft carrier HMS *Formidable* was lost in the morning mist that rose from the surface of the sea.

In the cockpit of the leading aircraft, Lieutenant Robert Hampton Gray peered ahead through the haze, searching for a glimpse of his objective: the coast of Japan.

It was the early morning of 9 August 1945. Just three days earlier, the first operational atomic bomb had obliterated the Japanese city of Hiroshima, and the Allies knew that the end of the long and bitter war in the Pacific was in sight at last. But the Japanese still had plenty of fight left in them, and the British and American carrier pilots maintained their non-stop offensive against the enemy's homeland, mercilessly hunting down the remnants of the once-proud Imperial Japanese Navy.

Robert Gray was one of *Formidable's* most experienced pilots. A Canadian – born in Trail, British Columbia, on 2 November 1917 – he had joined the Royal Canadian Navy's Volunteer Reserve on the outbreak of the Second World War, and in July 1940 he had come to England with seventy-four other candidates for training as possible officer material with the Royal Navy.

On completing his basic training as an Ordinary Seaman he was transferred to the Fleet Air Arm and sent back to Canada for a six-month flying course at Collins Bay, near Kingston, Ontario. He made the grade without difficulty and returned to England for operational training, after which he was posted to the East Indies Command. He spent the next eighteen months mostly in Kenya, with spells aboard the carrier HMS *Illustrious* on operational patrol in the Indian Ocean.

Then, in August 1944, he joined HMS *Formidable* as a fighter pilot with No. 1841 Squadron, which had recently re-equipped with the new and powerful Chance-Vought Corsair fighter. He was just in time to see some hectic action, for his carrier was part of a naval task force assigned to knock out the mighty German battleship *Tirpitz*, which was lying crippled in Altenfjord on the Norwegian coast.

The *Tirpitz* had been damaged by midget submarines in September 1943, but it could only be a matter of months before she was made seaworthy again, and if she escaped from her Norwegian lair she would wreak havoc among the Allied North Atlantic convoys. Naval dive-bombers had already attacked the great ship in April, but although they had inflicted further damage on her they had not succeeded in putting her completely out of action. Now, four months later, the Germans had built up a formidable array of anti-aircraft defences around the warship.

The task of the naval fighters was to 'soften up' the enemy flak positions scattered around the fjord, paving the way for the Barracuda dive-bombers. Every attack was a nightmare, the pilots running the gauntlet of murderous streams of fire as they raced low up the fjord towards their objectives. Time and again, Gray led his section into the attack, seeing their cannon shells blast great chunks from the rocky walls of the fjord and churn into the German gun emplacements. On one sortie, enemy fire shot away part of Gray's rudder, but he limped back to the carrier and made a successful landing.

Two bombs hit the battleship, but the dive-bomber crews were frustrated by the heavy smoke screen laid down over the anchorage and the *Tirpitz* escaped serious harm. She was later towed south to Tromsö for repairs, and it was there, in November 1944, that she was finally sunk by Lancasters of RAF Bomber Command.

Gray's part in the *Tirpitz* attacks earned him a Mention in Despatches for 'undaunted skill, courage and determination'. Not long afterwards, *Formidable* left home waters, bound once again for the Indian Ocean.

Early in 1945 she sailed for the Pacific to join Task Force 57, a force of five British carriers under the command of Admiral Sir Philip Vian which was working alongside the United States Navy in the assault on the last Japanese-held islands. In April, *Formidable* and the other carriers went into action against Japanese airfields on Sakashima Gunto. There was little opposition from enemy fighters, but the following month Gray and the other new arrivals had their first taste of Japanese fanaticism when the Task Force was attacked by twenty suicide aircraft. The Fleet Air Arm fighters shot down several of the attackers, but two got through to their targets. One bounced off the armoured deck of the carrier *Indomitable* and the other hit *Formidable,* destroying eleven parked aircraft. Four days later she was hit again, a sheet of blazing fuel from the crashing Kamikaze wiping out eighteen more Corsairs and Avengers. The damage was quickly patched up, and operational flying continued almost unchecked.

By July 1945, the sea and air battle had moved into Japanese home waters. During this period, Gray led a series of air strikes against airfields in the Tokyo area and made several attacks on Japanese warships, sinking a destroyer with his 500-pound bombs in a daring low-level attack on 28 July. For these actions, he was awarded the Distinguished Service Cross.

After the strikes at the end of July, operations were delayed for nine days because of bad weather and the dropping of the first atomic bomb on Hiroshima on 6 August. The attacks on Japanese targets were resumed on the ninth, and at sunrise *Formidable*'s flight deck was a hive of activity as Gray's section of four Corsairs was armed and fuelled. At the briefing, Gray and the other three pilots were told that they had an important target. A reconnaissance aircraft had sighted Japanese warships at anchor in Onagawa Bay, on the coast of the main Japanese island of Honshu.

One by one, the four Corsairs thundered down the flight deck and formed up over the carrier before setting course. Within minutes, *Formidable* had been swallowed up in the haze.

Gray and his fellow pilots kept a watchful eye on the horizon. The Japanese still had quite a few fighters left, and they would go on defending their homeland to the bitter end. But this morning the sky was empty; everything was calm and peaceful, and it was almost impossible to believe that a war was still raging.

Suddenly, the misty outline of the Japanese coast loomed up ahead. The fighters were right on course. Gray brought them round in a wide, sweeping turn, looking down at the distinctive outline of Onagawa Bay. Intelligence had been right; there, floating at anchor, were the slender shapes of five enemy destroyers.

Gray ordered his pilots to circle overhead and cover him while he went down to the attack, then put his Corsair into a steep dive. Immediately, shells from dozens of anti-aircraft positions on the destroyers and around the bay converged on the plummeting fighter. Gray continued his dive, levelling out only when he was a couple of hundred feet above the water. At close on 400 mph he streaked towards the destroyer he had selected as his target.

Above him, two Corsairs began to strafe the Japanese gun batteries in an attempt to draw some of the deadly fire away from his aircraft. The fourth fighter continued to circle the bay keeping a lookout for enemy fighters. It was the pilot of this aircraft who, momentarily forgetting his task, had eyes only for Gray's speeding aircraft – and what he saw he would never forget as long as he lived. It was an act of cold-blooded, suicidal courage.

Gray's fighter was almost hidden by fountains of spray, whipped up by the vicious storm of shellfire. The Corsair was hit time after time and pieces began to drop away from it. Most pilots would have broken off the attack, but Gray flew on. It was not simply a question of bravery; it was something in Gray's character that compelled him to press on against overwhelming odds.

It was like the attack on the *Tirpitz* all over again, except that this time the lone Corsair was the target of all the guns the enemy could bring to bear. This time, there would be no flight home, no welcoming thud of undercarriage on deck and brutal deceleration as the arrester hook engaged the wire, no relaxing drink in the wardroom while the tension oozed away.

The distance between the Corsair and the enemy destroyer closed rapidly. High above, the pilot of the fourth Corsair saw flashes along the fighter's wings as Gray's cannon hammered shells into the warship's superstructure.

Suddenly, Gray's aircraft was enveloped in a brilliant glare. Lurid flames streamed back from its port wing as a

Japanese shell found the fuel tank. Yet still Gray bored in steadily, never wavering from his course.

The Corsair flashed over the destroyer like a fiery bullet. Its single 1000-pound bomb tore into the warship just behind the funnel. Instantly, the destroyer erupted in a vast cloud of flame and smoke, shot with the glowing trails of exploding ammunition.

Out of the other side of the towering, flame-streaked mushroom a burning comet emerged, a ball of fire that climbed steeply, trailing an oily streamer of smoke in its wake. It was Gray's Corsair. It reached the top of its arc, then, almost lazily, turned over on its back and plunged into the water in a shower of flaming debris. Only a patch of oil on the surface marked the pilot's grave.

With a scream of engines, the other three pilots dived and dropped their bombs on the remaining ships. Then, twisting and weaving through the savage fire that poured on them from all sides, they sped out over the open sea. Behind them, a pall of smoke roared skyward from the sheet of blazing fuel that surrounded at least two shattered destroyers.

The Corsairs landed on *Formidable* shortly before nine o'clock. At that moment, a solitary American B-29 bomber was heading towards the city of Nagasaki, the second atomic bomb nestling in its belly.

Six days later, with the enemy negotiating for surrender, all offensive operations against the Japanese mainland were suspended.

For his bravery, Robert Gray was posthumously awarded the Victoria Cross. He was the last man to re-receive the decoration in the Second World War.

DOOMSDAY MISSION

In August 1945, a small body of American airmen carried out the most fearsome bombing missions in the history of air warfare: the dropping of the first atomic bombs on Japan.

No bomber crews had ever faced greater uncertainties. Apart from the danger from the enemy, no one knew exactly what might happen when the terrible power of the sun was unleashed.

And when it was all over, the crews had to face the most terrible question of all – a question which, in its own way, demanded of them great fortitude and courage.

Were they among war's greatest heroes – or history's greatest mass murderers?

ONE DAY IN AUGUST, 1944, A TWENTY-NINE-YEAR-OLD USAAF Colonel named Paul Tibbets received an urgent telephone call ordering him to report immediately to General Uzal Ent, commanding the USAAF Strategic Air Forces HQ at Colorado Springs. Tibbets, after flying B-17s on operations over Europe for nearly eighteen months, had only recently returned to the United States to play a leading part in the operational development of the B-29 Superfortress, which was just beginning to roll off the assembly lines. He was recognized as one of the most experienced of American bomber pilots.

At Colorado Springs, Tibbets met Dr Norman Ramsey, a Harvard Professor and a specialist in ballistics research, and Captain William Parsons, chief of weapons development under a scientist named Dr Robert Oppenheimer at a remote research establishment in the New Mexico Desert: Los Alamos.

It took Ramsey and Parsons a week to turn Tibbets into a scientist. In a briefing that lasted several days he was initiated into the mysteries of nuclear physics, of the splitting of the atom and the undreamed of energies that were released as a result. He was told as much as he needed to know about Project Manhattan, the biggest scientific research programme every undertaken by mankind, of the efforts of thousands of scientists and engineers

163

all channelled towards one goal: the production of the most awesome weapon in the history of warfare, the atomic bomb.

Tibbets was not slow to grasp the enormity of what he heard, or of the task that lay ahead of him. No one knew yet whether the weapon would work, but if it did it would have to be delivered to an enemy target. That was Tibbets' job: to form a special bombardment group composed of the best air and ground crews the USAAF had to offer, and to train them to an unparalleled standard of skill and accuracy. The programme was to be known as Operation Silver Plate.

When he reported to Colorado Springs, Tibbets' new command existed only on paper. Its designation was the 509th Composite Group, and Tibbets was given a free hand in selecting the personnel for it. He also had to find a suitable training base, and set out in a B-29 to reconnoitre a list of possible locations. His eventual choice was Wendover Field, also known by the codename of Base W-47, which lay in a desolate, barren wilderness 125 miles west of Salt Lake City in the Utah Desert. It was as remote from civilization as the moon, and ideal for the 509th's top-secret purpose.

The next step was to recruit personnel: 1,500 of them from bases scattered all over the world. Tibbets quickly surrounded himself with a nucleus of known and trusted veteran crews, many of them fresh from the embattled skies of Europe. Ground staff with outstanding records, from crew chiefs to stores clerks, suddenly found themselves spirited away from appointments in other commands and posted to Wendover literally overnight; protests from senior officers were quickly silenced by telephone calls from the highest Air Force authority.

By the end of September 1944 the 509th was up to strength, with its full complement of officers and men and fourteen new B-29s. The Group was a fully self-contained unit, and security precautions were stringent in the extreme; FBI agents with top security ratings shadowed personnel in their off-duty spells and reported any irregularities they overheard.

The element of the 509th Group which would deliver the actual weapon to its as yet unspecified target was the 393rd Bombardment Squadron, and intensive training was well under way by the beginning of October. None of the crews had the remotest idea of what their eventual task was to be and there was widespread puzzlement over the nature of the training, which involved a weapon delivery technique totally different from anything previously employed.

Bombing practice, carried out over remote desert areas of the United States, always involved a run-in to the target – a white circle on the ground – at altitudes of not less than 30,000 feet. Great emphasis was placed on achieving the maximum visual bombing accuracy, something else that perplexed the bombardiers; over Europe weather conditions had led to the development of radar bombing techniques, and the weather was likely to be even worse over Japan.

During training sorties each B-29 carried one large, bulbous bomb weighing 10,000 pounds. Immediately on release, the pilots put on sixty degrees of bank and brought the bombers round through a 158-degree turn, heading away from the target area. The Manhatten scientists had calculated that this unorthodox technique would put a distance of eight miles between the B-29 and ground zero when the bomb exploded forty-three seconds after release, the bomber increasing speed in a shallow dive. To gain a few extra knots the bombers were stripped of all non-essential equipment and armament, retaining only the .50 machine guns in the tail.

In December 1944 the 393rd Squadron moved to Cuba, where it was to spend eight weeks. From here, the crews practised long-range sorties over the ocean, a sure indication that they would eventually move to the Pacific. Other training during this period involved rapid re-deployment of the 393rd and all its supporting equipment, always on a fully self-contained basis.

Meanwhile, development of the atomic bomb was proceeding at a fast rate, and by the end of December 1944 Brigadier-General Leslie Groves, in overall command of the project, felt confident enough to announce a timetable. In a memorandum to the US Chief of Staff, General George Marshall, he indicated that the first bomb ought to be ready by 1 August 1945. It was immediately apparent that the weapon would be operational too late to be used in the war against Germany, where the Third Reich was already on the brink of collapse, although serious thought had been given to using it against a German target – probably Berlin – if the war in Europe had been prolonged. Groves therefore suggested that the Pacific Naval Command be alerted and a base set up for the 509th from which its B-29s could reach Japanese targets.

In February 1945 Commander Fred Ashworth, who had been in charge of ballistics development at Wendover, flew to Guam to see Admiral Chester Nimitz, the Navy c-in-c Pacific. Ashworth carried a letter signed by Admiral Ernest King, Chief of Naval Operations, which explained the atomic bomb project and requested that Ashworth be given the highest priority.

The base selected by Ashworth was Tinian, in the Marianas, 100 miles nearer to Japan than Guam. A level limestone platform some six miles wide by thirteen in length, Tinian's very smallness made it ideal for the secret nature of the undertaking. Moreover, it had a network of good roads developed by the Japanese, and plans were already afoot to turn the island's North Field air base, with its four concrete runways, into the biggest bomber base in the world.

While hordes of us Navy engineers worked flat out to transform Tinian into an unsinkable aircraft carrier, development of the atomic bomb picked up speed in the spring of 1945, with the reactors at Oak Ridge and Hanford already producing Uranium 235 and plutonium in small quantities. The designs of the atomic bombs were also being finalized; the uranium bomb was nicknamed 'Thin Man' after President Roosevelt, while the more bulky plutonium bomb was named 'Fat Man' after Winston Churchill. Later, when the gun barrel of Thin Man was shortened, the bomb was renamed 'Little Boy'.

In March 1945 the 509th Group returned from Cuba to Wendover for more trials over the deserts of the western United States. The bombs they used this time featured the finalized design, with live charges of high explosive, and the fall of each missile was recorded by cameras and scientists who accompanied every training sortie.

On 5 April the us War Department approved the code-name 'Centreboard' for the mission of dropping the atomic bomb on Japan, and later that month eight hundred men comprising the advance party of the 509th embarked from Seattle for Tinian, followed by the first B-29s early in May. The unit's arrival on the island was greeted with an announcement by 'Tokyo Rose', the Japanese equivalent of Lord Haw-Haw, but after that the enemy ignored the 509th, believing it to be a conventional bomber unit.

The 509th was separated from other air force units on Tinian by barbed wire and armed guards. The other units regarded the newcomers with some scepticism, particularly when the weeks went by without the 509th taking part in the strategic offensive against Japan. Instead the

Superfortresses of the 393rd Squadron flew lone sorties out over the Pacific to one of the islands still held by the Japanese, where the B-29s would release a single 10,000-pound bomb, painted bright orange and nicknamed the 'Pumpkin' to be detonated in the air over the target. As the summer wore on, some of the crews wondered if the 'Pumpkin' was really the end product of all the months of arduous training.

Most, however, were content to await the big mission which they were sure was on the horizon. They were still waiting when, on 16 July 1945, the first experimental plutonium bomb was detonated in the New Mexican desert. Five days later, one of the 393rd Squadron's crews – No. 15 in a B-29 nicknamed 'The Great Artiste' – dropped a 'Pumpkin' over the marshalling yards at Kobe and swung away in the evasive action they had perfected over the preceding months. The next time crew No. 16 returned to Japan, it would be to make history.

On 4 August 1945, seventy officers of the 509th Group were called to a special briefing on Tinian. The room was darkened, and a film projector whirred. In the minutes that followed, they saw the fireball of the first atomic bomb flare out over the desert, dragging its poisonous mushroom cloud. Now, for the first time, they realized the significance of their extraordinary training programme.

From among those seventy men would be selected the crew that was to drop the first operational atomic bomb. The following morning – a Sunday – scientists on Tinian began to assemble the components of Little Boy, which had been shipped out a few days previously and had been held under heavy guard – for their final journey. From five possible targets—Kyoto, Kokura, Niigate, Hiroshima and Nagasaki, Hiroshima had been selected to receive the most awesome weapon ever devised by man. The drop was to be made on 6 August.

For the sortie – designated Special Bombing Mission No. 13 – seven B-29s were allocated. One would drop the fourteen-foot, 10,000-pound bomb; the rest would provide a backup force and carry out photographic and scientific observation work over the target.

At seven twenty-five on 6 August, a weather reconnaissance B-29 radioed that conditions over Hiroshima were good. Its coded signal, which read simply 'Advice: bomb primary' was picked up by the B-29 captained by Colonel Tibbets and carrying the atomic bomb. Until that moment, Tibbets had been prepared to divert from Hiroshima and bomb one of the two alternatives, Kokura and Nagasaki.

Tibbets' B-29, named Enola Gay after his mother, had taken off from Tinian's coral runway at two forty-five, followed by two other Superfortresses – one of them Major Chuck Sweeney's 'The Great Artiste'. Their task was to make a photographic record of the mission and to measure blast and radiation. Another B-29 was standing by at Iwo Jima to transfer the bomb from Enola Gay if the latter developed technical trouble.

At four fifty-five Tibbets made rendezvous with the two B-29s that were to accompany him and the trio set course north-westwards in a wide V formation towards the Japanese island of Shikoku. As they made landfall over the enemy coast, tape recorders plugged in to the B-29's intercom system began running. 'This is for history', Tibbets told his crew, 'So watch your language. We're carrying the first atomic bomb.'

At nine minutes past seven the weather reconnaissance B-29, far ahead, made the first of its two runs over Hiroshima before heading out to sea. In the city, the all-clear sounded. The sky was a brilliant blue; although the rest of Japan was overcast, Hiroshima was surrounded by a ten-mile break in the clouds.

The crew of Enola Gay sighted the city at nine minutes past eight as the B-29 droned over Shikoku at 31,600 feet. The target showed up crystal clear in the sights of Major Tom Ferebee, the bomb-aimer. There was no difficulty in picking out the aiming point, the centre span of a bridge over the Ota River. At eight fifteen plus two seconds Ferebee initiated a radio tone signal, indicating that the bomb would be released in fifteen seconds. The crew pulled on their special goggles; the lenses, coated with quinine crystals, were designed to exclude every colour except purple.

At eight fifteen plus seventeen seconds Ferebee pressed the bomb release and the B-29 leapt as its 10,000-pound load dropped away. Tibbets immediately went into a tight turn to starboard. Two miles away, Major Sweeney also turned away in the Great Artiste and dropped a package of instruments.

In Tibbets' B-29 the crew mentally ticked off the forty-three seconds to detonation. In front of the console that monitored the bomb's circuits, First Lieutenant Morris Jeppson watched the count reach forty-two seconds and, for a wild moment, thought that the bomb was going to be a failure.

Far below, at an altitude of 1,870 feet over the city, nine and a half pounds of cordite inside the black and orange body of Little Boy exploded and drove two chunks of uranium together with the speed of a bullet. In a millisecond, Hiroshima ceased to exist.

The interiors of the three B-29s were lit up by a brilliant purplish-white flash that momentarily blinded some of the crew members, even through their protective goggles. Over Hiroshima, a fireball expanded to a diameter of 1,800 feet with incredible speed; the temperature at its centre was a hundred million degrees Fahrenheit. As Tibbets dived away from the target, a visible shock wave raced out from the explosion at the speed of sound, striking the B-29 with the force of a large flak shell bursting close alongside. It was followed by another a few seconds later.

With the immediate danger over, the three B-29s turned south and flew over the outskirts of Hiroshima, their awed crews watching the great mushroom cloud that raced straight up to a height of four miles. Hiroshima itself was invisible under what looked for all the world like a sea of boiling ink, spreading out from the base of the pillar of smoke. Beneath it, 70,000 people were dead or dying.

The B-29s turned away on the long flight back to Tinian. Tibbets broke radio silence to send an uncoded message back to base: 'primary target bombed visually with good results'. No fighters, no flak. The first part of the 509th's secret mission was over.

In the two days that followed the destruction of Hiroshima, B-29s of the US 20th Air Force dropped more than sixteen million propaganda leaflets on forty-seven Japanese cities, urging rapid surrender. It was also decided in Washington to bring forward the date of the second atomic bomb mission, originally scheduled for 11 August, to the ninth. The day before, Major Sweeney took the 'Great Artiste' out over the Pacific and released a dummy bomb into the ocean; it contained all the component parts of Fat Man except for the plutonium core, and the fuses, switches and detonators functioned without a hitch. It was the first time that the components of the plutonium bomb had been assembled inside the casing.

At eleven o'clock in the evening, the crews of the Great Artiste and two other B-29s assembled in the briefing room on Tinian. A map on the wall indicated the primary target; Kokura, in northern Kyushu. Nagasaki, on the west side of the island, was the alternative. For this mission the Great Artiste would once again be the instrument aircraft, as it still contained the special equipment fitted for Hiroshima; it would be flown by Major Fred Bock. The latter's aircraft, nicknamed 'Bock's Car', would carry the bomb and would be piloted by Sweeney. The third B-29, commanded by Major Jim Hopkins, was to carry film cameras and a team of British observers, including Group Captain Leonard Cheshire.

Preliminary weather reports were far from good. A typhoon was reported in the vicinity of Iwo Jima, which meant that the three B-29s would have to rendezvous off Yakoshima, a small island south of Kyushu. By that time, weather reconnaissance aircraft should be in a position to advise on conditions over the primary and alternate. Under no circumstances was the bomb to be dropped other than by visual aiming.

As the crews prepared for take-off, a serious snag was revealed in Bock's Car. The auxiliary transfer fuel pump in the lower rear bomb bay had gone u/s, which meant that 600 gallons of gasoline – the B-29's reserve – was trapped. Despite this, Sweeney decided to press on; there was too much at stake for the mission to be postponed, and they could land at Iwo Jima to refuel on the way back.

At one fifty-six, Japanese time, Bock's Car rumbled down Tinian's runway and lurched into the air, held back by the full load of fuel and the weight of the bulbous bomb. The bomber climbed steadily to 31,000 feet, passing Iwo Jima. A solid carpet of cloud stretched beneath it. At seven forty-five Yakoshima was sighted through a break in the cloud and a few minutes later the first weather reports came in from the reconnaissance aircraft over Japan. Conditions over both targets were much the same: hazy, clearing rapidly, with two-tenths cloud cover. Almost perfect for the mission.

At nine minutes past eight Bock's Car and the Great Artiste made rendezvous and the two aircraft circled over

Yakoshima to await the third B-29. Forty minutes later, however, the third aircraft had still not appeared. Sweeney, not daring to delay any longer, set course for Kokura, the primary target.

The initial run-in to the target was made by radar, the bomb-aimer taking over as the city came within visual range. There was no difficulty in picking up landmarks; the river that flowed past Kokura was clearly visible, as was the network of streets. Only one thing in the city was invisible, obscured by industrial haze and smoke from a large fire: the aiming point, a large Japanese Army arsenal.

Sweeney flew over the city three times while the bomb-aimer tried to get a visual fix on the target, but it was no use; the arsenal remained hidden from view. Japanese flak was now bursting dangerously close, and Sweeney's radio operator was picking up chatter on the enemy frequencies which indicated that Japanese fighters were climbing to intercept. The decision was made; the bomb would be dropped on the alternative, Nagasaki.

With its fuel situation already becoming serious, Bock's Car droned away towards the new objective. There was only enough gas in the B-29's tanks for one run over the city, and even then it would barely have enough left to scrape into Okinawa. To make matters worse, as the bomber approached Nagasaki the crew saw that the city appeared to be covered by nine-tenths cloud, instead of the anticipated two-tenths. Sweeney, by now thoroughly tense, made up his mind to drop the bomb by radar – contrary to orders – if the aiming point could not be picked out visually.

With only thirty seconds to go the bomb-aimer finally sighted Nagasaki through a gap in the cloud cover. Through it he picked out the outline of a stadium; it lay one and a half miles northwest of the actual aiming point, the commercial area near the harbour, which was still obscured by cloud. By way of compensation, the bomb-aimer asked Sweeney to make a slight correction to the right.

The bomb was released at eight minutes past eleven, Japanese time. Forty-three seconds later, the fireball erupted at 1,540 feet in the sky over Nagasaki and the awesome pillar of smoke climbed like a tombstone through the clouds that shrouded the Urakami Valley.

As he turned away from the shattered target, Sweeney sent a signal to Tinian: 'Bombed Nagasaki 090158z visually with no fighter opposition and no flak. Results technically successful but other factors involved make conference necessary before taking further steps. Visible effects about equal to Hiroshima. Trouble in airplane following delivery requires us to proceed to Okinawa. Fuel only to get to Okinawa.'

Twenty minutes after the bomb went down, another B-29 arrived over Nagasaki. It was Major Hopkins' aircraft, which – hopelessly lost over Kyushu – had been nearly 100 miles away when the crew saw the flash of the exploding weapon. It circled Nagasaki at 38,000 feet, the great mushroom cloud towering above it for another 20,000 feet, while its film cameras rolled. Hopkins then set course for Okinawa.

Far ahead of him, Bock's Car was in trouble. Arriving over Yontan Field on Okinawa, Sweeney was unable to make radio contact with the ground. By this time both Sweeney and his co-pilot, Captain Albury, were practically exhausted after some twelve hours at the controls and the B-29's fuel warning lights were glowing. There was no time even to make a circuit.

As the B-29 bored in towards the runway, Sweeney ordered his crew to fire off every flare on board. On the ground, an airfield controller noticed the multi-coloured display and warned a formation of B-25 bombers in the circuit to hold off. The B-29 hit the runway halfway along its length at 120 mph and slewed to the left as two of its fuel-starved engines cut out. It plunged on, its two remaining propellers howling in reverse pitch, and came to rest on a taxiway. Two hours later, Sweeney and his crew completed their journey to Tinian, arriving at ten twenty-five to face a barrage of interrogations.

For Major Charles Sweeney, however, the real interrogation came when, a little over four weeks later, he walked through the devastation of what had been Nagasaki together with his bomb-aimer and co-pilot. They had sown the wind; would the rest of mankind be left to reap the whirlwind?